Money Mavericks

FT Prentice Hall
FINANCIAL TIMES

In an increasingly competitive world, we believe it's quality of thinking that will give you the edge – an idea that opens new doors, a technique that solves a problem, or an insight that simply makes sense of it all. The more you know, the smarter and faster you can go.

That's why we work with the best minds in business and finance to bring cutting-edge thinking and best learning practice to a global market.

Under a range of leading imprints, including *Financial Times Prentice Hall*, we create world-class print publications and electronic products bringing our readers knowledge, skills and understanding which can be applied whether studying or at work.

To find out more about Pearson Education publications, or tell us about the books you'd like to find, you can visit us at **www.pearsoned.co.uk**

Money Mavericks

Confessions of a Hedge-Fund Manager

Lars Kroijer

**Financial Times
Prentice Hall
is an imprint of**

PEARSON

Harlow, England • London • New York • Boston • San Francisco • Toronto
Sydney • Tokyo • Singapore • Hong Kong • Seoul • Taipei • New Delhi
Cape Town • Madrid • Mexico City • Amsterdam • Munich • Paris • Milan

PEARSON EDUCATION LIMITED

Edinburgh Gate
Harlow CM20 2JE
Tel: +44 (0)1279 623623
Fax: +44 (0)1279 431059
Website: www.pearsoned.co.uk

First published in Great Britain in 2010
© Pearson Education Limited 2010

The right of Lars Kroijer to be identified as author of this work has been asserted
by him in accordance with the Copyright, Designs and Patents Act 1988.

Pearson Education is not responsible for the content of third party internet sites.

ISBN: 978-0-273-73198-6

British Library Cataloguing-in-Publication Data
A catalogue record for this book is available from the British Library

Library of Congress Cataloging-in-Publication Data
Kroijer, Lars.
    Money mavericks : confessions of a hedge-fund manager / Lars Kroijer.
        p. cm.
    ISBN 978-0-273-73198-6 (pbk.)
    1.   Hedge funds.   2   Hedge funds--Management.   3.   Speculation.   I. Title.
    HG4530.K76 2010
    332.64'524--dc22
                                                                                2010019032

10 9 8 7 6 5 4 3
14 13 12 11

Typeset in 10pt Galliard by 30
Printed and bound in Great Britain by Ashford Colour Press Ltd, Gosport, Hants

To Puk, Anna and Sofia – my three girls

Contents

Acknowledgements

As a first time author I probably needed more help than the journalists and professors that often write about finance, and I am thrilled that such an insightful and helpful group of people helped me to finish the book. In particular I want to thank my wife Puk Kroijer and good friend James Hoffman for their unwavering support throughout this project. Also, I would like to thank the team at Pearson Education for taking on the book and helping to shape it into what it has become: my editor (and fellow QPR supporter) Rupert Morris who wielded the knife gently, but also Chris Cudmore, Melanie Carter, Jane Hammett and Anna Campling.

A number of finance and non-finance friends read through early drafts of the book as I stumbled towards a coherent story and gave great and astute feedback: former officemate Edwin Datson, former colleagues Brian O'Callaghan and Sam Morland, but also early backer Martin Byman, and Christina Type, Oliver Emanuel, Curt Peters, Robert Sherer, Chris Rossbach, Tets Ishikawa, Marc Sharpe and Martin Escobari. Also, particularly in the early stages of the project while I was still debating if there was a story here to tell, I found the encouragement and direction from author friends invaluable, in particular Jeremy Dann, Kaleil Isaza Tuzman, Nalini Kotamraju and Kambiz Foroohar.

Finally, I would like to thank all those in and around the hedge-fund industry who consistently encouraged me to write about my experiences, even if those often included themselves. Most were content for me to use their real names, but some preferred to remain anonymous – with the result that some names and exact circumstances have been changed. The general feeling was that the world could do with a better understanding of what really happens inside hedge funds (and perhaps, just as importantly, what doesn't). Any industry that is this consistently open and encouraging of an introspective story about it can surely not consist only of locusts and speculatory leeches on society.

Lars Kroijer
May 2010

Introduction

This is the story of the life of a hedge fund. I started Holte Capital in 2002 and returned all the external capital to the remaining investors in February 2008. Those six years tested my sanity and resilience to their limits. In this book, I want to explain what it was like to run a hedge fund during a period where the industry went from relative obscurity to something everyone's uncle would discuss.

When I set out to write this book it was mainly because I felt the inner workings of the hedge funds were poorly understood by outsiders. Having grown from a small and mainly US investment activity to become a global trillion-dollar circus, the industry is often unfairly portrayed as a fee-charging gambling den populated by dart-throwing chancers and Bernie Madoff's evil twin. This was nothing like the industry I had been a part of for a decade and I recognised little of my time at Holte Capital in many of the accounts. The industry I had known largely involved highly intelligent people who were passionate about the world of investing. They would spend endless hours engaging in complex financial analysis to find angles from which their investors might profit. If they failed, the repercussions would be swift and severe. If they succeeded, the rewards would be massive by any normal standard – probably too big. It was certainly exciting, but not in the way most people seemed to think.

The term 'hedge fund' is often thrown around as if we all know what it is, or are meant to know. To me, hedge funds constitute investment funds that invest in a very broad array of assets classes, often across multiple geographies, and with very different risk profiles. Sometimes hedge funds are extremely narrow in their strategy while many engage in multiple strategies within the same fund. Like a mutual fund, the hedge fund manager charges an annual management fee, but in addition charges a performance fee on profits. The performance fee is typically where the really big bucks are made. The investors in hedge funds may be wealthy individuals, but more

often they are institutions such as banks, endowments, insurance companies, or funds of funds, all trying to capture returns that are not dependent
on market movements (funds of funds are exactly that: funds that invest in
hedge funds). In the media, hedge funds are often made out to be reck-
lessly risky ventures that day-trade stocks, and while some are undoubtedly
just that, more are in fact much lower risk than the general stock market,
and frequently hold securities for years. As you would have guessed, a
hedge fund uses hedges such as selling borrowed shares or buying protection to guard against things like stock market declines, credit defaults, or
similar – thus hedge funds. Wikipedia does a good job of describing hedge
funds if you want to dig deeper.

My own introduction to hedge funds came while I was at Harvard
Business School. Up to that point, I'd been following a well-trodden
finance path: a major in economics at Harvard University followed by a
hard apprenticeship with Lazard Frères working in investment banking in
New York. It was an unusual experience for a Danish boy from north of
Copenhagen but, in general, the rules, process and path of a banking career
were well understood and somewhat predictable. Hedge funds, it seemed,
were very different. I attended classes by Robert Merton, who had just won
the Nobel Prize in economics for his work in options. Merton was already
famous for developing the Black–Scholes–Merton option-pricing formula
and was getting even more attention for the phenomenal returns of Long
Term Capital Management (LTCM) where he was a partner. I knew him
well enough to go to his office and ask him about hedge funds. The meeting was inconsequential, as he could only vouch for LTCM, and they were
not hiring at the time. LTCM collapsed soon afterwards with multi-billion
dollar losses (described in Lowenstein's excellent book *When Genius Failed*)
and Merton was widely derided as the public face of the failed hedge fund,
even though his day-to-day involvement had been limited.

In my view the demise of LTCM did not make hedge funds a bad thing
per se. On the contrary, the more I looked at this type of investing, the
better it looked to me. A bunch of very smart people were trying to do
something that was incredibly hard: beat the market. They were using tools
from disciplines such as finance, economics and mathematics that I really
enjoyed working with. They cared about how things really worked – companies, industries, economies, societies and, not least, market and human
psychology. I saw it as the study of real life, with the market representing

the sometimes unfair but always ruthless arbiter – an arbiter who would mainly reward high-quality work and punish imposters. The hedge-fund industry struck me as a place where the no-bullshit rule would prevail and meritocracy ruled.

Depending on the definition of hedge funds, the industry has been around for decades, but really started to take off in the mid-1990s to manage around $2 trillion today before gearing, depending who you ask (down about 25 per cent from the peak before the 2008/9 turmoil). The industry grew as individuals and institutions increasingly opened their eyes to what were seen as uncorrelated returns that would earn them a profit even in a bear market. Asset growth really took off as larger institutions accepted hedge-fund allocations just as they had allocations in private equity or other asset classes. It seemed a good idea to allocate at least some assets in investments that could be expected to do well in falling markets. As some of the earlier hedge funds had stellar returns that appeared uncorrelated to the wider market, the investment opportunity attracted ever increasing numbers. Obviously many (including myself) saw this growing investor base as an opportunity to set up new funds to meet the increasing demand. And with the larger asset base, some hedge funds became quite powerful and active in the management of household company names. Being opaque organisations and with unknown fund managers, the funds were seen as dark forces of cynical capitalism at its worst, and they were often viewed negatively by the few in the general public who even knew what they were.

I saw those who were running hedge funds as money mavericks in the sense that they operated at the forefront of a rapidly developing and unpredictable part of the financial industry. They had strong, driven personalities and did not care about conventions: dress code was irrelevant, age did not matter, blue-chip employers were no guarantee. The only thing that mattered was whether you could create great profits given the risk you took for your investors.

My own first step in hedge funds was with a New York-based value fund which went from $600 million to $40 million in assets under management soon afterwards (nothing to do with me, but then they all say that). From there I went back to Europe and joined the multi-billion dollar fund HBK

> The hedge-fund industry struck me as a place where the no-bullshit rule would prevail and meritocracy ruled.

in their London office to invest in merger arbitrage situations. After agonising over the decision to quit, I left the relatively safe confines of HBK in spring 2002 to set up Holte Capital. So, soon after my thirtieth birthday, I was taking on the world of finance with an old college buddy – hubris to say the least

I hope that a takeaway for readers of this book will not be that all hedge funds are like Holte Capital. They are not. In an industry that is as diverse in investment style and personal characteristics, generalisations are often misleading. Yet the Holte Capital story includes many factors symptomatic of the industry in addition to the firm's own fate. It is a story of naivety, rejection, hubris, bubbles quickly inflating, arrogance and occasional hatred. At the same time it is one of success, ambition, friendship, courage and love. Sadly for my publishers, and unlike some accounts from the financial world, there are no excesses of sex and drugs. The Holte story does not include $20,000 bottles of wine and endless lines of cocaine, and in my years in finance I have seen virtually none of it elsewhere. What I have seen a lot of is dramatic events, sometimes played out in seconds, but more often extended over longer periods of increasing stress. I often feel that my six years of running Holte Capital was one long blur of human drama, with triumph and failure following each other in quick and merciless succession. If you have ever been given the impression that the world of hedge funds is driven by meticulously planned and well-coordinated dark forces, I hope my story will enlighten as well as entertain.

> If you have ever been given the impression that the world of hedge funds is driven by meticulously planned and well-coordinated dark forces, I hope my story will enlighten as well as entertain.

PART ONE

Getting ready for Holte Capital

1

Becoming a hedgie

Good luck, Lawrence

Hedge funds had not yet exploded onto the scene in 1998, when I was in my second year at Harvard Business School. By contrast, Internet start-ups were all the rage. Why bother with cash-flow analysis and five-year projections when you could help change the world while living in sunny California? It may have been a failure of imagination on my part, but I had spent my summer working at the private equity firm Permira, and that seemed like my best option. I had worked at McKinsey too, but management consultancy wasn't for me. So there I was, vaguely thinking about going into private equity, when my friend, Dan, who would later found a multi-billion-dollar hedge fund, proposed that I meet up with a couple of hedge funds he knew. The same week, one of my professors suggested that I might enjoy working with the multiple financial instruments that hedge funds provided.

I duly sent off my résumé to the hedge funds Dan had suggested. I had little idea of what they did, other than that the people involved were an aggressive and nasty bunch. I remembered being a 22-year-old investment banker at Lazard Frères in New York where I had hung up the phone on a couple of super-aggressive investors who wanted to know more about my deals. My boss had told me to ignore them. 'They are just hedge funds,' he said – as if they had some contagious disease. I now know they were merger arbitrage investors, simply trying to get an edge on a specific deal.

My first meeting was with Richard Perry of Perry Capital at his New York offices. Richard Perry was and still is one of the titans of the hedge-fund industry, running multiple funds well into the tens of billions of dollars. He was already a billionaire himself several times over, but I had never heard of him and my attitude was 'Let's see if what this guy has to say is interesting enough to warrant a look', in typically arrogant business-school style. My attitude, embarrassingly, represented the near-epitome of Harvard Business School self-importance where I expected others to assume I was brilliant and immediately offer me a suitably paid job.

I was thoroughly unexcited about the prospect of meeting Perry. The type of merger arbitrage analysis I remembered from Lazard felt like a peculiar brand of aggressive investigative journalism, so I expected an office with holes in the carpet and people shouting obscenities into the phone and at each other. I imagined Perry himself to be a short, fat, balding chain-smoker. Instead, I was led through artfully decorated offices to an executive-style conference room at the opposite end of the large floor. Perry himself was also a surprise – a tall, tanned and handsome man who clearly looked after himself.

He was eloquent and suave, apparently genuinely interested in my background and family in Denmark and my amateur golf career. He smiled at my well-rehearsed jokes and anecdotes as though he had not heard similar ones a thousand times before. But I could only pretend to know about him and hedge funds for so long.

'So what do you know about us?' he asked after the initial niceties.

'Not much to be honest. I'm just starting to learn about the hedge fund industry. Both a friend and a professor of mine suggested that there could be a good fit between what you do and my interests.'

'But do you know what we do?' asked Perry, slightly puzzled.

'Well, I know you invest mainly in public market securities like stocks and corporate bonds and aim to create absolute returns. I imagine you use a fair bit of derivatives for hedging purposes which I am interested in, having written my thesis on equity call options.'

In other interviews, my thesis on equity derivatives had counted for something, but not here. Perry nodded like a teacher who had just given me a C, but was willing to give his student another shot.

'Do you have any stocks or investments you think are particularly interesting?' he ventured.

'Not really, to be honest,' I replied, completely missing the opening he had generously handed me. 'I haven't really been following the stock market closely. I figure that stock markets are pretty efficient and if you are going to have any chance at all to beat them you need to commit to it full time with access to the best information. If you don't, it might be better to put your money in an index fund. Or hedge fund, obviously,' I added, quickly remembering where I was. This was the equivalent of a car mechanic saying he is not really interested in cars or a vet saying that animals are an unnecessary annoyance.

Perry's response was measured. 'There's probably some truth in that, but most people who work here have a long history of investing in the stock market and a genuine interest in it.' He was trying to reason with me, but I was oblivious to his openings and stuck with my 'Why don't you tell me why this is interesting?' attitude.

Richard Perry had clearly picked the wrong guy to spend 30 minutes with, but he bravely gave it one last shot – albeit with increasingly evident annoyance.

'So you don't have a natural interest in the markets and you are not familiar with us or the work that we do. Do you mind telling me why you sent us a résumé?'

'Well, I am very interested in investments in general and have some experience in private equity, which I found fascinating. It sounds like this meeting might have come a bit early in my exploration of the industry, but I was keen to hear the views of a hedge-fund manager before deciding on career choices,' I said with the blithest arrogance.

'Why don't you go away,' said Perry, 'and figure out if hedge funds are for you and what you want to do. We can take it from there.'

'That sounds good. I will be back in touch if I take that route,' I said, as if the decision were mine and not his. He looked incredulous for a moment, then shook my hand and said, 'Good luck Lawrence' as he handed me back my résumé. Ouch. I was about to say 'It is Lars – I am Danish', but thought better of it and mumbled my thanks to Perry as he walked out the door.

In the course of that interview, Richard Perry taught me two lessons that stayed with me long after the pain and embarrassment had receded:

1 Don't be an arrogant prick. I had had a run of job offers when I met Perry and thought I walked on water. When self-confidence becomes arrogance, you deserve to be shot down.

> When self-confidence becomes arrogance, you deserve to be shot down.

2 Negative feedback can be positive. The bluntness with which Perry shot me down spiked my interest in the industry that would dominate my life for the next ten years.

A year later, I met Richard Perry again. I reminded him of our unfortunate first meeting and told him how it had inspired me to learn more about hedge funds and become more humble.

'That was one of the worst interviews in my 20 years of doing this,' he said with a knowing smile. I'd like to think it was my worst, too.

Back to base

I was shell-shocked after the Perry interview. Two years into business school, I felt as if I had met endless private-equity investors, consultants, investment bankers and Internet entrepreneurs, and generally had a good idea of the work they did. There were hundreds of job postings in more than enough industries and countries to satisfy any student's ambitions. With the Internet really starting to take off, many 'bricks and mortar' companies thought hiring business-school students would help them to meet the challenges of the new economy. Many students juggled four or five job offers. Others were planning to start their own Internet-related businesses and it seemed everyone was scouring the campus for people willing to be number two in what would surely be the next Microsoft (this was pre-Google, of course).

I remember sitting in a class where Amazon CEO Jeff Bezos came to speak to 70 students to discuss company strategy. The next year, his speech filled the largest auditorium on campus with overflow screens in the adjacent building! With the number of students trying to become entrepreneurs right out of university it was as if the start-up risk was lower than usual. If your venture failed (as many did) there was a long line of well-funded ex-classmates, eager to hire someone who had already been on the front line of the Internet revolution. You were also thought to be cool for having even given it a shot.

I did not think this world was for me, though. I reasoned that those who were likely to do best out of the new technology would have a combination of business savvy and technical skill, and although I might have had the former, I was sorely lacking the latter.

Hedge funds were different and far more opaque. There were no job postings for hedge funds in the career service's bazaar, nor a category where you could look up people in the alumni database and ask their advice about the industry while dropping not-so-subtle hints about finding a job.

I had duly joined the investment management club the previous year but only had a T-shirt to show for my $50 membership fee. I naïvely hoped that listing my membership on my résumé would signal that I was a born winner in the investment management game. I slowly began to build a picture of the work and of the main players in the industry. The general feedback from the guys (there were virtually no women in the crowd) was similar: their jobs were not very structured, there was little hierarchy, skill was enthusiastically acknowledged by superiors and lack of it punished mercilessly. The job was entrepreneurial, in that you were encouraged to pursue what you thought were interesting angles, and if you were good the money was great. It was also clear that the type of work varied quite a bit from fund to fund. While the fixed-income or statistical arbitrage funds could be very mathematical in nature, the work at some of the long or short funds largely resembled that of more traditional stock-picking.

Joining the clan

I eventually joined a value fund in New York called SC Fundamental. During the interview process, the firm's founder, Peter Collery, had thoroughly impressed me and I still consider him one of the smartest people I have ever met. Value investing is basically the art of paying 50 cents for something that is worth a dollar, and the firm often focused on unsexy securities that were trading too cheaply compared with their tangible assets and often boring earnings outlook. Peter had been in the value-investing business for many years and had a great track record, a $600 million firm and significant wealth of his own. Not that you could tell from looking at him. Tall and skinny with large round glasses, Peter would wear the same worn-out trainers, threadbare jeans and crumpled shirt every day. In my first interview, he immediately pulled out a thick 10-K report (an extended version of an annual report) and asked me what I thought about a particular exhibit. The exhibit detailed how this life-insurance company accounted for the long-term liabilities of potential workers' compensation claims and

> It may sound sad that two grown men could sit in an office and get excited about long-term liabilities of an insurance company, but it was kind of fun.

how it matched these by holding certain assets against them. Peter was looking for me to say there was a mismatch, since the present value of the liabilities was lower than it immediately appeared. It may sound sad that two grown men could sit in an office and get excited about long-term liabilities of an insurance company, but it was kind of fun. This was not investing with buzzwords, drama and sweeping judgements – Peter would not know a buzzword if it hit him in the face – but instead was more like puzzle-solving and discovering things that others had missed.

I accepted the job with SC Fundamental mainly because of Peter. He said they wanted to exploit new markets and he would like me to open a London office in two or three years' time if things were going well. This appealed to me. I would be paid $100,000 a year and guaranteed a bonus of the same amount in my first year. Quite a step up from Lazard. Another thing that had appealed to me was the absence of boiler-room talk that I had encountered elsewhere.

One guy had sat me down in his office and stared at me in silence for about a minute before saying: 'Lars – do you wanna be rich? Like really rich? I have a collection of old cars and a $20 million Hamptons mansion down the road from Mary Meeker and I can make you rich', before telling me about his day-trading scheme. By contrast, Peter seemed like a studious investor who loved the research process and matched his analysis with market savvy to make a lot of money for his investors.

Happy that I had found the right job, I graduated from HBS in the summer of 1998 and went off to spend a few months in Argentina to teach a bit and learn some Spanish before I was due to start at SC Fundamental in the fall. But things are never that easy. While I was working my way through endless bife lomos and vino tintos in Buenos Aires, the partnership broke up as one of the three partners wanted to leave to set up his own firm. This turbulence coincided with a period of underperformance at the firm and SC Fundamental had a much more dubious outlook.

On the morning of my first day, Peter and I had a friendly introductory chat. The past year had been tough for the firm both because of partnership bickering and also because of the cost of some of the fund's short positions in what we considered over-hyped Internet companies. It looked like this was going to be the first down year for the firm. Peter felt let down by some of the investors who had made good money with him over the years only to redeem their investment at the first drawdown. Over a 12-month period two-thirds of the assets had disappeared.

Unusually for an analyst right out of business school, I was given my own office (I have not had one since, in fact). The office was a couple of floors above the fancy private-wealth managers from UBS who undoubtedly thought Peter with his 'homeless chic' look had got through security by mistake. As this was my first foray into active asset management I was initially unsure of how to start tackling the analysis of companies. Without really thinking, I started to build 30-page Excel models with elaborate forecasting using assumptions plucked from thin air. Peter looked at the endless small black numbers on the printouts and soon started to rip the model apart by asking, 'Where does this assumption come from?' This taught me my first lesson about using massive investment-banking-type financial models in hedge-fund work: the technique could work, but you needed to be constantly aware of bullshit in/bullshit out syndrome.

I was enjoying feeling close to the front line of investing. At Lazard I had become a machine that could spit out endless financial models without having to think much about what the company in question actually did, whereas here it was all about what the company did and its outlook. At Lazard I would frequently put together presentations in a frenzy, only to be asked to stay behind at the office instead of being invited to the meeting where the real action was. At SC Fundamental, I wasn't just a member of the team – I *was* the team. The progression from idea to investment was simple and direct: find the trade → do the work → talk to Peter → do the trade.

Unfortunately, my time at SC Fundamental ended before a year had passed. Those 'over-hyped' Internet shorts kept rallying and in the first quarter of 1999 the fund was down 14 per cent after being down 6 per cent for the year in 1998. Even though I agreed with Peter's value arguments, it was hard not to be disillusioned by the lack of results. As a friend put it, 'The Internet is going to change the way we live for the better and you want to bet against that!?'

The remaining investors seemed to agree with my friend and mercilessly redeemed virtually all the external capital, leaving Peter and a few friends as the only investors. The fund was down to $40 million in assets and there was no point in keeping the whole team of 10–12 professionals, so Peter told us to start looking around for jobs. He had not yet decided if he was going to keep going, but if he did it would just be him with the support of a trader and his old friend Neil, the CFO.

Although I have fond memories of my short time at SC Fundamental, I was surprised at how quickly the investors had turned their backs on us. If the firm was judged so harshly for a 15-month bad run after 10 years of good performance it was no wonder that most hedge funds were looking for near-term returns. Any step off the straight path to profits would clearly be severely punished.

More interviews and sharp objects

Within a year of leaving HBS I was back on the job market – like more than 50 per cent of HBS graduates, who leave their first job within a year. At this stage I had lived for close to a decade in Boston and New York, and I decided to give London a try. My original plan had been to spend three or four years in New York after business school, then head to London with SC Fundamental, but the firm's early demise ruined my plans. I thought 1999 was a good time to make the switch, both because London was starting to boom financially, and for more personal reasons: it would allow me to be closer to my family, and my new Danish girlfriend (now my wife), Puk, would be more comfortable there.

Although SC Fundamental may not have ended with the success that the quality of its work seemed to merit, there was a great list of former workers there who had gone on to start successful hedge funds and were happy to talk to me. Through this network of friends of friends I ended up having coffee with the New York power broker of start-up hedge funds, Dan Stern, of Reservoir Capital. In less than 30 seconds, it was clear that Dan knew just about everyone worth knowing in the community. I was about half a minute into my pitch about why I enjoyed hedge funds when Dan held his hand up as if he was stopping traffic.

'You don't have to bullshit me,' he said. 'You don't want to work here. We are a seed-capital fund, and I don't think you would fit anyhow. Why don't you just tell me what you want to do and I'll think of some people for you to talk to?'

I was slightly annoyed by his comment. Although my pitch to potential employers was obviously designed to make me look as good as possible, it was also fundamentally honest. In my short career I had seen the inside of investment banking (Lazard), consulting (McKinsey), private equity (Permira), and hedge funds (SC Fundamental) and while two of them had only been summer internships I felt I knew a fair bit about the various industries and was making a well-informed decision in only looking at hedge funds. I told Dan that, boring though it may have sounded, I was telling him my real thoughts. I added that I had always wanted to be an entrepreneur and could eventually see myself starting my own hedge fund if the opportunity presented itself, but that this would not surprise anyone. Dan looked at me again and smiled. 'Hang on a minute', he said and picked up the phone to dial 'a friend'.

'Hi Larry, it's Dan,' he said, and smiled at a joke cracked at the other end. 'Listen – I have a young guy in my office who wants to work for a hedge fund and would prefer being in London. Are you guys looking? Yeah, I know you're always looking for the right people, but would this fit?' Within about two minutes, Dan had set me up with an interview with Larry Lebowitz at HBK Investments, a Dallas-based hedge fund with a stellar reputation and returns, and, importantly, an office in London. Three minutes later, he had organised a meeting with Dan Och of Och-Ziff, another leading hedge fund in New York that was considering opening a London office. 'Who needs a headhunter when you have Dan Stern?' I joked to a friend on my way out.

After spending a day at HBK meeting with all the senior staff, I was asked to spend a day in London for interviews with the two heads of the four-person office there. In Dallas I committed another excruciating interview faux pas: I asked the founder Harlan Korenvaes where the name HBK came from. Luckily he thought I was joking, smiled and said: 'Well, you will not be shocked to hear that my middle name starts with a B.'

On the day of my overnight flight to London I was sitting in my midtown office, leaning back in my comfortable chair and mindlessly scratching the inside of my ear with a pen while reading. All of a sudden I heard a small 'pop' in my ear and pulled out the pen, embarrassed at my idiocy and carelessness. It didn't hurt too badly and I thought no more about it as I headed to the airport. On the flight across the Atlantic my ear started to itch badly, and so I started to scratch it with another pen. It didn't help.

Although I was starting to have trouble hearing, I went to meet Sam Morland who was head of risk arbitrage and inter-capitalisation trades in Europe, and Baker Gentry, head of convertible bond trading. With his Texan background, Baker was clearly the 'company man' of the two.

Sam was soft-spoken with a mild demeanour that concealed his strong intellect and curious mind. Too embarrassed to tell him what I had done, I told him I had a bad ear infection (which later turned out to be the case) and that if I seemed to be ignoring his questions it was just because I could not hear a word. Sam smiled, said something I couldn't make out, and gave me a series of math/finance quiz-type questions, obviously reasoning that the language of mathematics did not require hearing. Baker asked more general questions about my background and interest in HBK. He told me how he had started the office in London and although he worked mainly with convertible arbitrage they were more interested in me for risk arbitrage and special situations trades. 'Not that I have ever come across a situation that did not think it was special,' he added with healthy scepticism. I liked the atmosphere and thought I had a good rapport with Sam, who would be my new boss.

As the day progressed, my ear deteriorated. It was soon clear that I was going to need medical attention, but I put it off. As I headed to Heathrow for my return flight, my ear was throbbing with pain and I debated for a minute whether I should go to the emergency room before boarding the plane. The next eight hours on the plane in seat 47F sandwiched between a sumo wrestler and the undoubted winner in a recent '40 hotdogs in 30 minutes' contest was agony. My ear felt like a gaping wound into which someone was sticking a thick needle with easy passage to my brain. I took to asking everyone around me for painkillers and when one kind soul offered me some Tylenol, I emptied half the container into my hand and promptly swallowed five of the sixteen tablets I would take on that flight. The pain subsided slightly as my world became increasingly blurry, and I took to chewing the tablets to get the drug more quickly into my bloodstream.

On arrival at Kennedy Airport I took a cab straight to the emergency room on 12th Street near my apartment on Bedford Street in the Village. The receptionist asked the obligatory 'Are you in pain right now?' and without waiting for an answer sent me back to one of the examination rooms. The young doctor who came to look at me half-laughed as he asked me, 'How on earth did you do this?' and called over a couple of colleagues to show them the damage. He told me that I had managed to give myself an inner and outer ear infection and also burst my eardrum. 'No more deep-sea diving for you,' he joked as he handed me a small container of liquid medicine. As I poured the liquid in my ear I could feel it passing through the hole in my eardrum and into the back of my mouth with a disgusting disinfectant taste. I was discharged around 3am and with a new set of elephant-strength painkillers I went home and slept 14 hours straight.

A week later I was back in good health and thrilled when HBK offered me a job to start as an investment professional. Over the past seven days I had lost any hope of becoming a scuba-diver, but gained a job in merger arbitrage and special situations investing. London beckoned . . . and I was eager to follow my new calling.

2

Taking the plunge

Joining 'The Firm'

HBK was founded in the early nineties as a convertible arbitrage shop. Harlan Korenvaes had used his connections from heading the convertibles group at Merrill Lynch to raise money for his own venture. Since inception, the returns had been excellent. After the early days of focusing on one area, the firm had quickly expanded into others such as fixed-income arbitrage, merger arbitrage, emerging-markets fixed-income, and special situations. When I joined in July 1999, the firm was managing around $1.5 billion in assets, on its way to managing double-digit billions five years later. There were eight partners at the firm when I joined, along with a whole army of people in back offices for a total headcount of around 150. The firm made a point of being discreet about its existence – over the years I came across many people even inside the hedge-fund community who had never heard of HBK, although it ranked among the world's largest and best performing funds.

With the Internet bubble popping in 2000/1, a lot of new merger-arbitrage analysts had to look elsewhere to make money. Good merger-arbitrage analysts are often not good value investors and don't have a lot of experience at valuing companies in the typical investment-banking fashion. This was where I thought I could provide an angle to make some money for HBK and myself. From my time at Lazard and SC Fundamental I had experience with fundamental value analysis and could use this skill now. I began to work more on situations where there was not only value analysis, but also what we called an 'event' – a catalyst that might help realise profit. This could be a spin-off where a company was selling a division and I had to value the remaining entity; it could be a merger or some other change in the shape of a business, or a tax ruling that could affect the overall value of the company, or any number of other situations. I found myself enjoying this combination of analysis tremendously as it played to my skills and interests both in assessing the likely impact of the 'event', and also in looking at the value and prospects of real businesses.

Although Sam was a great boss and a fantastically nice guy, and although HBK was a world-class firm, it quickly became apparent that HBK was a part of my career journey and not my destination. I have always had the entrepreneurial bug and after about two and a half years at HBK I started to think about venturing out on my own.

Agonising decisions

My plans to start my own hedge fund really started to take shape during the late fall of 2001, after two years at HBK. I was just 29 and foolishly thought I knew almost all there was to know about investing. One evening, I sat down in my apartment with a blank piece of paper and wrote at the top: 'How to start a hedge fund.' I pondered for a while and eventually came up with four things I needed to figure out quickly to see if this was possible.

1　Team?

2　Strategy?

3　Investors in fund? Seed/non-seed?

4　Process and budget to launch? Timing?

The first two were the easiest. I had decided early on that I wanted to be the boss on the investing side. Although I knew a number of people who would be qualified and interested co-portfolio managers, I decided that I would not approach anyone at this stage. My experience from SC Fundamental led me to believe that partnership divorces are extremely costly and frequent in hedge funds. If I could wait until much later in the process to bring in someone to help with investing, I would not have to share quite so much of my business. And on the non-investing administrative side I knew I had my man – Brian O'Callaghan. Brian and I were close friends from our college days and had stayed in touch. We had originally met in an economics class in college and, after Brian asked me to join his fraternity (the Harvard term is a final club), we started to hang out more. After college Brian had been a consultant, then a broker, before starting an Internet venture that was slowly dying. I knew Brian was an honest, smart and hard-working guy who would be a perfect CFO. Of course, he had no experience with hedge funds, but I put that down as only a minor drawback! When I first talked to Brian about the idea he thought it was an exciting one, and immediately started to dig out information on how to get going. I knew even then that I was lucky to have him.

Strategy was easy. I would be doing a European market-neutral special situations fund. Today people at hedge funds would say, 'What, another one?', but at the time there were few small independent funds covering European special situations. Besides, it was what I had been working on since business school, so it made sense to continue to use this attractive market.

The tougher questions were 3 and 4. Investors? Hmmmm – oh yes. You mean those people whose money you will be managing for a large fee? In the months before launch, my own incredible naivety in this area would be made clear, but at this stage, absurdly, I did not consider it a big problem. I had seen friends raise crazy amounts of money for very dubious business plans in the technology space that went on to go bust. Unfortunately I did not come from a wealthy family, but I thought there was enough money among people I knew that I would be able to raise a good amount. I also knew that a lot of these conversations could only take place after I had left HBK. When I was free to talk to everyone I could approach the prime brokers; I knew they had special groups that solely existed to raise assets for hedge funds. I could also then explore the seed capital angle where one investor gives you a fairly large chunk of money and gets a stake in your overall business. One of my colleagues had told me after a few too many beers that a potential seed investor had promised him $75 million for 30 per cent of the business, and, while I didn't believe that for a second, it made me think, 'If he can get $75 million, I am sure I can raise $40–50 million.'

The process of starting a hedge fund is not that time-consuming. Assuming that you have passed the necessary exams (FSA registered in the UK or Series 7 in the USA) and can therefore execute trades on behalf of your new fund, all you need is to be approved by the FSA, which typically takes four months. Of course, a million things happen in between, but if you have money and FSA approval you should be able to fix those quickly. The costs were a bigger concern. In the previous two years at HBK I had been paid $600,000 a year, which was a lot for someone recently out of business school. But since the firm had set 40 per cent of the bonus to be paid over the next three years only if you remained at the firm and the taxman had already taken a good bite, there was not as much money left in the bank as the headlines suggested. Certainly not the kind of Monopoly money people would expect of someone about to launch a hedge fund. After a couple of weeks of research, Brian presented me with this diagram of what the structure would look like:

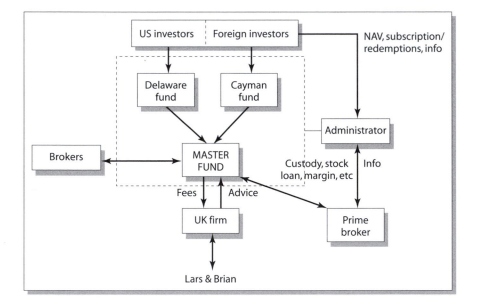

'Jesus, Brian,' I said. 'There's no need to make it harder than it is!'

'You kidding me?' he responded. 'I've left out about 90 things! Did you think this was going to be easy?'

'So how much is it all going to cost?'

'Well, the key thing is to distinguish between the fund and firm costs. The fund is where the investors have their money – this is a common master–feeder structure in which the Delaware and Cayman funds "feed" the master fund. Any expenses associated with the funds are borne by the investors and amortised over time. If we end up with no investors or not launching we will have to eat all the costs which will probably be around $250,000, mainly in legal setup fees,' Brian explained.

'In reality this is where they get you. When everyone is charging tons – and they all do – it is really the investors who pay for it. The administrator charges you a small fraction of your assets yearly, but if you don't have many assets this hurts since there are minimum fees. Also your negotiating position with the prime broker and execution broker is poor with low assets. Even though it is your investors who are paying, bad terms hurt performance and your ability to raise more money. It's a vicious circle. The UK firm is where we sit. This is where all the analytical work is done. In theory, we just advise the master fund on what to do, whereas in reality we control it so the things we want to happen actually happen. The costs at the firm will mainly be an office, Bloomberg terminals, IT and salaries.

'Did I mention salaries?' Brian joked. We had agreed that we would not be taking salaries until the fund launched, and after that we would scale them up as our assets increased.

'How much are we talking here?' I asked.

'Run-rate costs are probably $15–20K per month, but you have to worry about commitment periods. Even if we get a serviced office there will be at least a six-month notice period, and Bloomberg demand two years' commitment and you have to pay half the remaining costs if you cancel. You will also have to decide on things like if we should pay more to have real-time data feeds for share prices and so on. Then there are a bunch of up-front costs like computers, a server, accounting and settlement software, and travel expenses for marketing, but a lot of those prices have come down in recent years. We'll be fine if we allow $100K for all of that.

So you should probably count on a minimum spend of $150,000 at the firm, but also keep reserves in case we end up eating the fund expenses in a failed launch. Then there is of course the regulatory capital which the FSA require to just sit in a bank account in case we go bust – that's another $150,000 – it's not really an expense but it ties up capital. Also keep in mind that you will have to eat, so allow some money for personal expenses.'

Brian pulled out a simple summary of expenses we might include in an early draft of our presentation to investors:

Preliminary start-up budget (USD estimates)

Pre-investing budget*		First year running cost	
Legal & accounting	27,000	Bloomberg/Reuters	22,500
Rent deposit/estate agent	15,000	Rent charges	37,500
Hiring staff	7,500	Staff (2)	105,000
Furniture	3,750	Bookkeeper	3,750
Systems: hardware & software	45,000	External compliance	6,000
IMRO	5,063	Dedicated Internet line	7,500
Travel to market fund	45,000	Technical maintenance	7,500
Office expenses	7,500	Cleaning	7,500
Regulatory capital	155,813	Office supplies	30,000
	311,625	Travel	30,000
		Fees/expenses	15,000
			227,250

*IMRO fee based on standard £3,375

'So much for my savings!' I thought.

By early 2002, Brian was busy getting everything ready while I was still working at HBK. I did not want to leave my job before getting my bonus for 2001 and, to avoid the risk of Brian's enquiries revealing my intent to leave, he went into all the meetings describing me as a young hotshot who would join him in a couple of months. Brian would report on how many of the prospective service providers gave him a bored look and told him to come back when the mystery man was ready to come along, but he still got a good sense for who the main players were and what service pricing would look like. But without me being able to participate in the meetings it was hard to gauge how good our prospects were. Brian would explain my background in generalities and explain the strategy we planned to implement in broad strokes, but with half of the team missing, the whole thing looked a little like a dreamers' project that would probably never materialise. So we decided to chance it and both meet with one potential prime broker months before I would leave. Brian felt that his contact at Bear Stearns had seemed reliable and that Bear was a good, albeit second-tier, choice as a prime brokerage firm. We did not risk losing too valuable a counterparty if we came across as hopeless beginners for our first meeting, but Bear was also serious enough that we could use it as our prime broker if we really hit it off.

For our meeting with Bear Stearns, Brian had arranged to borrow a room in the offices of a friend's Internet company in a dark street off King's

Cross. Rather than taking time off, I had arranged for the meeting to be at 7pm and arrived 30 minutes early to strategise with Brian. As I walked down the quiet street, it was clear that we would not be selling ourselves to Bear with our choice of venue. The street contained a burned-out building, a tattoo parlour, a nasty kebab shop, a brothel and, naturally, a hedge fund start-up. I hoped we would look good in comparison. Tom was head of prime brokerage sales at Bear and was unfazed by the location. 'Don't worry,' he said calmly. 'The last meeting I had like this took place in a leaking houseboat.'

A master at selling, Tom quickly made us comfortable. 'Obviously,' he said, 'I am here to sell you on Bear Stearns and I would not be working there if I didn't think the offering we had was very good [soon afterwards he quit the firm], but you guys are not going to have a problem. There are so many banks that see Europe as the next large hedge-fund growth area. At this stage there are not many people starting funds with résumés as good as yours, so everyone will be willing to take you on as a client. Raising money will not be as easy, but since your prime broker will make more money the more money you manage, they will also try pretty hard to help you with this.'

> 'Well, I think we just lost our last excuse to not do this,' Brian said.

What a relief. We had spent a couple of months dancing around the issue of whether we would make it and here was a senior person at a large firm saying we were going to be fine.

'Well, I think we just lost our last excuse to not do this,' Brian said as we walked back to the train station.

Quitting

During the whole fact-finding period, when Brian and I had been making our initial enquiries, I had been longing to make the jump, but as the date for me to leave grew closer I found myself becoming nervous. I would be 30 by 4 February 2002 but still a spring chicken in the world of hedge funds. On top of that, I would not have a record I could take with me, and little tangible evidence that I could make money. The structure of the trades at HBK meant that, while I knew my own profit and loss, there was no separate figure for me and only the overall firm performance so I could not prove my results.

Days before I went to spend Christmas with my family in Denmark, Sam and Baker sat me down and gave me an excellent review and told me that my compensation for the year would be $600,000. But, in a twist that would set our launch back several months, HBK and its accountants had come up with a tax structure whereby employees would be paid through a system none of us understood too well. For reasons that they 'would not bore us with' we would only be paid the money in May or June, but would receive a legal document saying the money was ours in the next couple of months. Unable to say anything in the meeting that would reveal my intent to quit, I was fuming inside. I would now have to wait until I received the document or I might not get the money. The following weeks I dropped subtle questions asking when it might arrive, but Baker was clearly not too worried. 'It'll come soon,' he said with the voice of someone whose future at HBK was never in question. It was back to waiting while trying to keep our start-up momentum.

One Friday afternoon in March as I was leaving for a vacation, Baker asked for a minute in the conference room. 'You may not remember from your review,' he said, 'but part of the process for paying you the 2001 bonus involved giving you this paper saying that the money is legally yours. Anyhow, it's a minor point, but here it is.' And he handed it to me.

'Oh. Right. OK,' I said, as casually as I could. 'See you when I get back from skiing next week.' Inside, I was jumping for joy. Here was the permission slip to get on with my life that I had been waiting for since before Christmas. So now I had the document, what next? Now was the time when I needed to step up and prove to myself that I was ready for the future – ready to leave the cosy structure of overpaid salaried employment to pursue loftier ambitions with a high risk of failure. I felt I had been ready to leave for about a decade, but had somehow always found a convenient excuse to defer my dream. Now I was going to take the plunge.

A couple of days after I returned, I sat down with Sam to resign to him first. Sam was a fantastic boss and undoubtedly one of the hardest things about quitting was letting him down. Because my decision to quit had been floating around in my head for a while, I was surprised at Sam's shock at my decision. When I said the words 'I have decided to move on,' Sam did a quick shake of the head and asked me to repeat myself, thinking he had misheard me. I did most of the talking, explaining how I was going off to pursue a dream and that everything was only made harder by the fact that I was very happy working with him. Sam said that it sounded like I had my mind made up and, while he was sad to see me go, he understood what I was doing. Also, encouragingly, he said he was sure I would be successful.

The following day, I resigned to Baker. He was also friendly and said that since my mind was clearly made up, they would not risk bad blood by trying to persuade me to stay. When I returned to the trading desk, there was an eerie silence. It was highly unusual for me to ask for a meeting in the conference room with the two bosses, and when Baker asked Sam into the conference room to discuss what to do, one guy smiled and guessed, 'You just quit, didn't you?' I nodded and started to pack my things, trying to ignore the pregnant hush around me.

I walked down the stairs and out onto Davies Street, feeling liberated and slightly frightened. It was a beautiful spring day as I walked home through Hyde Park. It felt like a beginning rather than an end.

> It was a beautiful spring day as I walked home through Hyde Park. It felt like a beginning rather than an end.

Starting a hedge fund

World headquarters

By April 2002 we felt ready to forge ahead. We had already spent too much time looking like another set of would-be entrepreneurs at Starbucks who discuss world-conquering ideas over expensive skinny cappuccinos. The plan was to launch the fund in October when we had raised enough money. Brian was in charge of the practical aspects such as our FSA application, an office, technology, etc. It is actually a very simple business: we charge people to manage their money. We would charge 1.5 per cent of the invested amount annually plus 20 per cent of any positive performance we generated. The fee level was industry-standard (many charged a 2 per cent management fee), and trying to sell ourselves at lower fees would make us appear second-rate. On top of that, the investors would be charged for administrative, legal and research expenses as well as trading-related expenses such as brokerage costs, stock loan and so on. We had hoped to raise $40–50 million but appreciated that this could be harder than we initially thought – in hindsight, perhaps, the understatement of the century. At the $50 million mark, we would receive $750,000 in management fees every year and if we could generate 10 per cent gross returns, our incentive fee would be $1 million ($50 million × 10% × 20%). Not bad for a start-up. And you wonder why so many people try to start hedge funds?

The process is pretty simple too:

1 Get a team.

2 Get a prime broker.

3 Raise money.

4 Launch fund.

5 Buy securities that go up and sell those that go down.

6 Be rich, popular and happy.

How hard can that be? Predictably, not as easy as it looks.

I decided on the name Holte Capital for the company and fund, the name of the small town in Denmark I come from. I wasn't going to call it Kroijer Capital – how could the name of a 30-year-old portfolio manager with no track record convey experience, judgment and gravitas? In later years during rare business meetings in Denmark, the name Holte would earn me sceptical glances as my meeting companions naturally assumed I represented a tiny investment firm from a small suburb north of Copenhagen. But the name made it feel like our firm and it was great to have no higher power to answer to.

Without a real office to work in and still using our old home computers, the whole project still felt unreal. Brian and I were working out of my West London flat. It was a great location, but the flat itself was nothing to write home about. There was a small crack in the corner of the single glass window of our office – we called it our world headquarters – so on cold days we turned up the electric heater to stay warm. On rare sunny days we would sit in the combined living/dining room/kitchen to enjoy the rays and in time we added a few coffee stains of our own. Since my girlfriend Puk worked from home too, it all got a bit too cosy sometimes. Brian would complain that with Puk around he felt unable to spend time in the toilet with the sports pages reading about Arsenal, his beloved football team. My cheap and humble abode might suggest that I am the genuine article as an entrepreneur, but in reality I am just tight. On my salary at HBK I could easily have afforded something much nicer, but being cheap is in my DNA. Puk kept complaining, 'What do you need all that money for? You're never going to spend it anyhow!'

We had installed a phone in the office/second bedroom so we could have a Holte Capital voicemail. Out of the blue, Sanjiv from Rosemary Asset Management called one morning. How on earth did he get our number? Sanjiv had heard that I had left HBK to set up a fund and he would love a quick call with me and the CFO – did we have 15 minutes now? Although I was still in the process of learning who the important investors were, Rosemary was a recurring name. They had about $10 billion under management and frequently wrote $50 million cheques. I was completely taken aback and said, 'Sure, let me get Brian,' before I had a chance to think and ask to call him back later.

'Brian – there is someone from Rosemary on the phone. Get in here already!' I yelled to Brian who was having a rare Arsenal moment in the loo.

'Shit, give me a moment!' Brian yelled back.

I un-muted the phone and asked Sanjiv if we could call him back in 10 minutes. 'Sure, but I have a meeting in 30 minutes,' he answered.

We scrambled to get all our stuff together. We had not yet met an investor and this would be our first proper conversation. We pulled all the pieces of paper we could find together, one pile for Brian with all the administrative work and another pile for me with trade-related things.

'Do you think he'll ask me about risk management?' asked Brian hesitantly.

'How would I know?' I replied.

Fifteen minutes later we were ready to call Sanjiv.

'Where's the conference button?' I hissed at Brian as the Rosemary receptionist picked up the phone.

'Sorry, wrong number,' I said and hung up after Brian gave me an annoyed look. I had bought one of the cheaper versions on the market and the damned phone did not have a conference facility!

'You are such an idiot,' I kept saying to myself – an often-repeated phrase at this point in my life – as Brian and I debated what to do next. Rather than delaying the call we decided to call Sanjiv back and tell him the conference function on the phone did not work – and that I would keep Brian here if Sanjiv had any questions for him. So I had my first investor call sitting on the floor – we would buy furniture the next day – while sharing the receiver with Brian with our noses almost touching. The call itself was as uneventful as the lead-up to it was frantic. Sanjiv was just curious about what we planned to do and when we would launch. Did we have a seed deal lined up or did we want to raise money ourselves? And who was our prime broker?

The prime brokerage dance

We always knew that our meeting with the Morgan Stanley prime brokerage team was going to be an important one. Morgan Stanley was the leading prime broker in Europe and would appear on the shortlist of any start-up hedge fund. We had heard from friends in the industry that their capital introductions team was among the largest and best known – and we knew that in the absence of a large anchor investor our survival might well depend on the prime broker's ability to connect us with sufficient potential investors.

Once your investors fill in the subscription documents, your administrator wires the money to a bank account where some of it is held back for fund expenses, but typically the rest goes to the prime broker. So at a basic level this money pays for the securities you buy through the execution brokers in the market. Obviously there are tons of banks in the world that can provide those basic services, but with the recent growth in the hedge-fund industry, some of the large investment banks undertook massive infrastructure investments to provide specialised services unique to hedge funds. Of all the things we needed six months before launching the fund, having a prime broker was the one we cared about the most.

> Of all the things we needed six months before launching the fund, having a prime broker was the one we cared about the most.

So it was with some apprehension that we went to our meeting at Morgan Stanley. This was 'game on', as Brian would say. As we left the Underground station at Canary Wharf the many towers served as a stark reminder that we had come to play with the big boys. Trevor, our contact from Morgan, enthusiastically greeted us in reception. He told us that he had lined up a couple of people for us to meet. In his early thirties and a touch overweight even for his stocky frame, he casually led us through a maze of what seemed like hundreds of work stations. We arrived at a large conference room with great views of Cabot Square and the waterways beyond. Trevor would later tell me that the higher-ups certainly noticed when someone like him brought in new business and he really appreciated me getting in touch. As Trevor went to get his colleagues, Brian and I exchanged glances. These guys might just be serious about Holte's prospects.

Trevor came back with a colleague. And another one. And another one. Then they started coming on their own, and by the time the last one sat down there were eight of them, including three managing directors. As the most senior person spoke, it was clear that they were trying to sell us on Morgan Stanley. They thought we had a real chance of raising a lot of money up front, that we were among the brightest prospects this year (it was still only April, mind you), and they were impressed that we had already done so much work – we had only put together a list of our expected service providers, a one-page description of what we were going to do, and our bios. I kept thinking, 'We are not that hot and I know it. Who are all these people that Morgan claims we are better than?' Half-way through the meeting, while discussing their ability to help us raise money, someone suggested that we come to their large annual fund-raising conference in Versailles in a week's time. 'Game on indeed,' I thought, and told them I would have to check my schedule before committing.

Our new friend Marty now led the charge and he would be responsible for closing the deal with Holte. In his early forties, Marty had come to investment banking and his role as head of European capital introductions fairly late. At around 5'11" Marty had the build of a swimmer and exuded energy. I already had the impression of a man in a hurry as if he were running out of time on a game show. Marty would become instrumental in raising capital for Holte and is a personal friend to this day. After the brief awkwardness of trying to shake six hands quickly after the elevator doors opened, Brian and I were back on the street surrounded by complete strangers in expensive suits.

For the first and only time, Brian and I high-fived. We had gone into the meeting thinking we would have to sell Morgan Stanley on taking us as a client, and left with promises of a substantial effort on their part if we appointed them. Confident that we had found the right prime broker, we walked back to the Underground feeling that we had walked into the lion's den and had not just survived, but thrived. We started to speculate that a bank like Morgan would not show that kind of commitment only to have their prospective client fail and might even back the client with their own money if need be – incorrectly, as it turned out. On the way back we spoke quickly and excitedly about the great future that lay ahead like out-of-breath young boys telling their mothers about the great goal they just scored. We felt a jittery sense of excitement and optimism.

Striving to do a thorough job, we saw nine potential prime brokers. As you would expect, there were substantial differences and some seemed not to compete properly. Most disappointing were Goldman Sachs, who gave us a 30-minute talk on how hard it would be for us to raise money, but said they would give it a shot if we picked them. Perhaps we just got in via the wrong contact, but there was no real commitment on their part to put us in front of a number of investors, so not selecting them was an easy decision. At least their unwillingness to blow sunshine up our asses was a useful blast of honesty. Some of the others seemed to know that they would be ignored if we were taken on by Morgan or Goldman and said so. 'Come and see us again once you need a second prime broker,' one said. In the end we had the market leader show us real commitment to help raise a good amount of money, and that was as much as we could have hoped for.

By the time I looked into my 'busy schedule' and let Marty know that I would be happy to come to Versailles, we had pretty much decided that we would use Morgan as our prime broker.

Keeping my head in Versailles

It was with some timidity that I arrived at the Trianon Palace for registration at the Morgan Stanley European Hedge Fund Forum. In an effort to save money, I had taken an early easyJet flight to Paris and the Metro system from the airport to Versailles. Afraid to look too cheap (even by my low standards) if I arrived at the Trianon on foot, I took a cab from the train station and pulled up just behind a group of luxury sedans.

'Ah, Mr. Kroijer, we have been expecting you,' said the concierge before directing a bellboy to carry the 10 lb bag of my finest clothing up to my room. The bellboy opened the Renaissance-style double door to reveal a stunning three-room suite. Each room was adorned with paintings of soon-to-be-headless French aristocracy and beautiful golden mirrors. There were several massive plasma screens, three times the size of my little TV at home, and a dining table which led to a sunny terrace overlooking the gardens and a field where horses grazed idly.

'And how many people will I be sharing this with?' I jokingly asked the bellboy. He looked like he was about to crack a joke, but thought better of it and left.

With two hours to go before the first part of the conference, I took a shower and sat down on the terrace to look at the programme. It occurred to me that I didn't know if Morgan were paying for this. I started to call the Morgan conference desk to ask but was afraid I would look like a hopeless and moneyless amateur. I called reception instead.

'No, Mr Kroijer, unfortunately the guests have to pay for the rooms themselves. Your suite will be 750 euros plus taxes.'

'Ah, just making sure,' I said, while thinking to myself, 'Shit, that's two grand for the two nights of the conference – enough to get us a Bloomberg terminal for a while.'

Since I had already showered and generally made a mess of the room, it was too late to check out without paying for the first night, but I decided to stay somewhere else for the second. After the evening's drinking and mixing session there was no way anyone would notice if I escaped and stayed at a budget hotel in town. For a tenth of the price and double the peace of mind.

The first session at the conference was not really for hedge-fund managers. This was a session where leading lights in the fund-of-funds sector discussed which managers would be hot over the next year. The crowd was dominated by men in sharp suits. Many seemed to have a look that said, 'Being a fund-of-funds investor myself, I obviously have a better view on this than anyone, but I'll still listen to you.' It was interesting to what extent the panel's conclusions depended on the market. One thought credit-related hedge funds would do well because of the increasingly easy availability of credit (if he had kept that view for four years and then reversed it he would have done very well, but I never heard of him again). Another thought markets were going to rally and that Germany in particular was due a period of outperformance. I remember thinking that if they were able to make consistently correct predictions, they would be the richest people on earth – but they weren't. Not all of them anyway.

After another couple of sessions, most people had arrived and the networking was in full swing. The worst times for me were the 15-minute breaks in the anonymous conference halls during the panel sessions where you were clearly meant to be talking to someone or mingling. Standing alone in the hallway reminded me of high-school dances when all your mates had run off. I made a point of getting in the longest line at the coffee stands so it would take me longer to get my coffee and reduce my time alone. Once or twice I caught sight of some of the Morgan people I recognised from our meeting but they always seemed to be deep in discussion with someone about something hugely important. Eventually, Marty saved me. 'Why are you standing here alone? People should be swarming around you like bees to honey!'

He introduced me to a couple of friendly potential investors and soon I was one of the ones in the middle of a seemingly urgent discussion. For the first time I found myself selling Holte Capital. Since we were not yet authorised by the FSA, I was not allowed to formally market the fund but these casual chats were fine. So John, who was a former colleague of Marty's and now at a fund of funds, became the first potential client I had met. While I had expected to talk in depth about the intricacies of our analysis or how our hedging profile would enable us to get a unique return profile, the first series of questions were more administrative in nature.

Who is your administrator?
We don't know yet.

Will you have a master–feeder structure?
I think so . . . absolutely we do.

Who are your lawyers and prime brokers?
We don't know yet, although Morgan is clearly in the mix.

How much do you expect to launch with?
Perhaps $45–50 million?

What is your strategy?
We are a market-neutral special-situations fund. We will look at complex corporate structures where, through the hedging of one or more components, we can create exposure to some sort of residual business or asset that we can then go either long or short. So our analysis will consist of both value and catalyst approaches.

John interrupted me. 'That all sounds very interesting, but I have to run to a meeting with a manager. Let's chat more later on?'

Fortunately, my chat with John had caused a friend of his to come over and say hi and I got to repeat my spiel with him and another guy after that. When I was in the middle of having the same conversation for the third time, the hallway abruptly emptied. Apparently a panel discussion with the hottest manager at the conference was about to start and nobody wanted to miss it. Stupidly feeling that I should not acknowledge this guy's brilliance by being in the crowd at his discussion, I walked to the toilet with the pace of someone who is late for an urgent meeting.

I felt exhausted. Clearly this was going to be a couple of days' worth of elevator pitches, and I was woefully unprepared. I made a quick call to Brian and we agreed to appoint a lot of our service providers on the spot. At least that would take those questions out of the equation and let me move on to the investing aspects faster. We could always change the service providers if they turned out to be crap and Brian had done so much work on the initial list that we were basically there already.

Later that evening, there were cocktails followed by dinner at one of summer palaces adjacent to Versailles. Marty introduced me to Ebba who would be our special contact in the capital introductions group. There was no slight in Marty passing us on – he was responsible for several accounts already including several multi-billion-dollar funds. Ebba was a stunning six-foot Swedish woman who reminded me of the blonde from Abba. Annoyingly I could not help humming the tune 'Money Money Money' in my head when I met her. Ebba was clearly used to fighting to be taken seriously in a world where there are few women. My concern with her was more mundane. Would she be able to generate the introductions we so badly needed?

At the reception before dinner, Ebba did a decent job introducing me to potential investors even though she often had to introduce herself as well. The setting was stunning – the summer palace's terrace overlooked a botanical garden that oozed tranquility and peace. Flowers of all colours decorated the gardens below and surrounded a rectangular water fountain. Most of the guests were clearly happy to be there. For many, the conferences were an opportunity to catch up with old friends and gossip while also scoping out potential investments. As many of the fund-of-funds investors stood together, clearly the idea was to be involved with the fund they were talking about.

Being pre-launch added to the difficulty in evaluating Holte. Once our fund was up and running, the numbers would tell enough of the story that any half-sophisticated investor could talk about them at a cocktail party. For a start-up fund with no track record, this was harder. As a potential investor you would have to know something about the investment strategy of

> I knew our strategy was good but had no proof of my own skills.

the fund before gossiping about its prospects, or at least fall back on the background of the manager. I knew our strategy was good but had no proof of my own skills.

The reception was coming to a close and I had momentarily lost Ebba in the scramble to get a good table. I was looking around for her or someone else I thought it would make sense to sit next to, but found no one. Alone again. This reminded me of a wedding where there were no assigned seats. You know that your evening can depend on who you sit next to and if you get a bad table the whole thing can be terrible. Well, in the context of this investor conference I got the equivalent of the children's table. There were about 40 tables of eight and there were clearly going to be empty seats at the back. I introduced myself to the two youngish guys already at the table. They were friendly enough but clearly there to have a piss-up on an expense account. They were Greek and better dressed than me by a couple of grand. Each. One said he focused on distressed debt and his eyes glazed over when I tried my pitch to him. I soon gave up. The other one didn't really bother telling me what he did and soon resumed talking to his mate in Greek. Someone else sat down, but quickly excused himself when he saw a better table across the room with someone he knew.

The evening was not looking like a breakthrough event for Holte, and I briefly considered going back to my room and ordering room service. Two middle-aged Asian-looking guys sat down and made typically formal introductions. At least they made an effort to be nice to the lonely no-hoper. But sadly I could hardly understand their heavily accented English. 'Ah, start-up. Good. Good. Fixed income bad. Macro good,' and so on. After establishing that they mainly invested in macro, and only in managers who had been running for three years, I realised that they would also rather talk to each other. So there I was as a social outcast who ended up drinking too much of the lovely red wine. Half-drunk and half-way through dessert, I excused myself to join some people who had retired to the terrace to smoke. I don't smoke, but would have inhaled anything to escape that dining table.

Ebba caught up with me there. 'Where were you? Marty and I saved a seat at our table for you with a couple of investors in start-ups.' I tried to cringe only inwardly. After dinner, we walked through the park back to the hotel bar where an after-party of sorts was gathering. Nobody there seemed to want to discuss the finer points of hedge funds, but rather drink expensive whisky on Morgan's tab.

'You have great prospects!' one half-drunk guy told me, while wink-ing at Ebba. 'As a hedge-fund manager obviously!' he said before roaring with laughter. As if I had somehow missed the joke. 'Anyhow, they treat you like royalty here at Versailles, don't they?' he said as the waiter poured more champagne. 'Would that be before, during, or after 1789?' I thought to myself. I know which I felt like. I soon retired to my expensive suite annoyed with myself for drinking too much.

The next day of the conference was the day when a number of one-on-ones were set up. The various fund-of-funds investors could request meetings with the hedge-fund managers in the separate conference build-ing. As I was not allowed to have meetings like that, I quickly found myself doing more speed walks to the bathrooms pretending to be busy and gen-erally looking forward to lunch.

Loitering in the hallways proved quite effective in terms of meeting potential investors. There seemed to be an unwritten rule whereby people would smoothly rotate their conversations. After speaking to someone for two minutes, they would usually catch the eye of someone they knew who would stop by and take over the next two-minute interval. Of course, I was always quick to point out that I could stand in the hallway chatting only because I was not allowed to have formal marketing meetings yet – again the pending FSA application. The implication was that once I was free to market Holte Capital there would be a line out the door of people wait-ing to give us money. If only. The problem with loitering outside was that my scarcity value was plummeting. How hot could I really be if anybody who wants to talk to me can for as long as they like? So, in the afternoon I made myself scarce and went for a nice long walk through the gardens of Versailles, losing myself in the stunning surroundings and allowing myself to forget for a minute how desperately I wanted this to go well.

For the conference's grand finale, dinner was held at another summer residence in the Versailles gardens, and, although there were meetings the next day, the atmosphere was jovial and self-congratulatory. There were constant bursts of laughter from the scattered groups of three or four. Having done my hallway stint for a couple of days I found it easy to find people to chat to without Ebba.

As the scramble for the best seats began, Marty pulled me aside. 'You are sitting over here,' he said, and pointed to the centre of the room. About five tables were reserved and my seat was right in the middle. The gentleman in the next seat introduced himself and seemed surprised when I asked him to repeat his name as I failed to hear it in the general murmur of the dining hall.

'Byron Wien,' he said. The name did not ring any bells. We had a very nice conversation about Boston and he even expressed interest in what we were trying to do at Holte Capital. Although I could not place him in the hierarchy of Morgan Stanley it was clear by the constant interruptions from people who wanted to say hello that he was a man of considerable importance. My suspicion was confirmed when, after a brief introduction that included words like 'sage' and 'Morgan's answer to Warren Buffett', my dinner companion got up to be the evening's, and the conference's, keynote speaker with his apparently famous top ten list for predictions over the next year.

'Morgan must consider you a super-important prospect to sit you next to Byron Wien,' the nice man from Oxford on my other side noted. I just smiled and felt like an idiot yet again.

Getting our house in order

Back in London, Brian and I had expanded our team from two to three with the addition of Massimo Conti whom I knew from Harvard. Massimo was originally from Italy, but because of his father's job he had lived in Germany for many years and spoke fluent German. After graduating from Harvard and taking the obligatory two-year stint at a New York investment bank, Massimo had joined a large private-equity firm in London. Massimo's Italian roots had clearly left their mark. He dressed far better than Brian and me, with expensive shirts and designer jackets. As a former European wrestling champion, he had a good athletic build even if the years had added a few kilos in less desirable places. He had perhaps been told a few too many times that he was smart, and took great offence at suggestions he was anything short of a genius. But in many ways he was ideal for us, with a perfect résumé, private connections and strong analytical skills.

Massimo was clearly keen to break out from the normal corporate mould and try something entrepreneurial, so the fit was almost perfect. Understanding that the early phase was all about raising assets, he managed to get David Rubenstein (the head and founder of Carlyle) to stop by our humble office and, while he did not invest with Holte, we greatly appreciated having a heavyweight like Rubenstein consider us. Although a bit on the small side, we thought a three-man team was enough to start the fund. Without Massimo on the investing side of the business, Holte might have looked too much like a one-man band and, while his presence may not have added much in terms of investing experience, it gave us more of a team feel – if only on paper.

Brian was now busy with administrative things such as setting up our new office and starting the computer systems. With Massimo busy working on a portfolio of trades I had put together for him, I found myself in an oddly quiet period. This had to be the calm before the storm. Anticipating a rush to visit and invest money with us, we moved out of my flat and into 'real' office space in Mayfair in central London. Our new office at 23 Berkeley Square was just big enough to fit three desks and a café-style conference table in the corner. Massimo and I arranged our desks so we faced the wall sitting next to each other but were separated by a third desk which stuck out from the wall and served as a common area where our shared Bloomberg terminal sat. This was before Bloomberg required fingerprint login to ensure firms like ours could not share a terminal.

Across the 12 by 15 feet office, Brian had made a little corner where his desk would face the door and give the appearance of a separate operations division. The wooden panels on emerald walls had been painted gold by the gay-scene-focused headhunting firm that had the office before us. Since we were not keen on spending money refurbishing the space, we grew to like this kitsch display, especially as we were only paying £2,000 a month, having been given a discount because of the office's unconventional decor. Cost concerns had put us on the elevated ground floor and we could just see the tops of people's heads as they headed down Bruton Place to the local pub. Directly across the narrow road was a dark red stone wall and only if you looked at a certain angle out of the window could you catch a glimpse of Berkeley Square.

Berkeley Square felt right at the heart of the European hedge-fund universe. With beautiful imposing trees and a gravel path lining the inside of its black cast-iron fence, the square is the epitome of old-world charm. Someone once told me that Mayfair and St James manages more money than the entire city of Frankfurt, and although it is probably an urban myth, a London-based hedge-fund manager could easily believe it. Since the architecture of centuries past does not allow for the large-scale complexes needed by the big banks, the area lends itself well to smaller office spaces. While Holte Capital did not yet have anything to invest, we thought the right location would give the impression that we were a natural part of the hedge-fund scene. We might have saved £500 per month in rent in the City or Canary Wharf, but if that was going to tip the budget we would be toast anyway. We felt that if our location were to encourage just one more investor per quarter to stop by our office, it would be worth it. Besides, it was a nice place to work.

4

On the road

Following the impressive showing at Versailles and general eagerness to help us when we needed it, we quickly decided that Morgan had shown belief in us, commitment to making us a success, and that they would be our only choice as prime broker. When we called back the other potential prime brokers, nobody showed much surprise and most were quite gracious, although Goldman gave us a bit of the 'nobody turns down Goldman Sachs' attitude, saying they could not believe it.

Although our large pre-appointment conference room overlooking Cabot Square was replaced by a windowless room, Morgan's promise of commitment was quickly converted to real effort. We would plan a large road trip with stops in London, Paris, Geneva, Zurich, Milan, New York, Boston, Chicago and San Francisco. We could also do stops in Asia and the Middle East, they said, but in reality they typically invested in European managers through funds of funds or their regional offices if they had them. 'Cool,' I thought, 'I already feel like a rock star.'

The idea behind the road trip was simple. Morgan would use all its marketing connections in the various cities to put Brian and me in front of a series of investors whose profiles suggested that there might be a fit. We would aim to have six meetings per day and a dinner on the evenings when we were not travelling. Being in London was an obvious advantage. The city was quickly becoming a hedge-fund centre on the scale of New York, and most serious international investors would either have an office there or at least visit frequently. For us, this meant that we would not necessarily need to take all possible meetings during an already busy road trip, but could take some over a longer period of time in our office in London.

I could just imagine poor Ebba on the phone trying to fill our schedule: 'Yes, I *know* these guys don't have a track record and have never managed a portfolio before, but . . . yes, there *are* only two of them on the investing side at the moment, but they are thinking about lining up another analyst...'. We hoped her ability to attract attention in person would translate to the phone.

Our first two days would be in Paris. A frequent visitor to Paris all my life, I had always associated the city with romantic weekends and peaceful strolling on the lovely boulevards. This would be different. Brian and I ran from meeting to meeting and our morale declined as the day progressed. While our pitch was still not completely smooth, people clearly understood what we were doing, but kept coming back to a couple of key things. Did we have a track record? (no) and did we expect the fund to close at launch? (also no).

'As much as we like you and what you are trying to do, it will just make more sense to wait three to six months after launch to invest . . . but please put us on your mailing list,' they would say, as if this conveyed genuine interest. Although predictable, such remarks raised issues that we knew we would have to address if we were to raise money when launching the fund in the fall. Although it was hard to know for sure, we felt we could invest approximately $250 million with our strategy before we had to rethink or find extra liquidity. If the fund grew in assets to this amount very quickly, it would make sense to close it to new investors. On the other hand, if there was no such explosion of interest, fear of missing out would not be enough to persuade others to pile in. The lack of track record was an even more obvious hurdle to overcome. For all our fancy graphs and talk, we could not prove that we had done anything like this before.

From Paris we travelled by train to Geneva, then Zurich, where the next morning we left our one-star hotel and walked slowly towards the Hauptbahnhoff and the financial firms beyond. We had our usual pre-meeting prep talk: don't be too humble. Be confident, but not arrogant. Make them believe we have a number of investors lined up, but don't lie about anything. Be honest if you don't know the answer to a question and be sure you know that answer before the next meeting. We are good. We are

> We are good. We are smart, and we are the right people to be doing this. Just give us time and we will prove the doubters wrong.

smart, and we are the right people to be doing this. Just give us time and we will prove the doubters wrong.

All pumped up, we arrived at our first meeting. Our destination was a nondescript apartment building with a photo shop on the ground floor. Not fooled by this typical Swiss understatement, we pushed the buzzer for the fourth floor and went up. The office was nice, with dark wood floors and anonymous art on the walls. In the reception area were the usual *Financial Times*, *Fortune*, *Wall Street Journal* and a couple of art and sailing magazines.

'Must be for their rich private investors,' I whispered to Brian.

'Mr Gross will be with you in a minute,' the receptionist said as she took our order for coffee. My third cup of the day and seven more meetings to go – I made a mental note to cut down my caffeine intake.

Mr Gross turned up in a pin-striped three-piece suit with shiny brown shoes, gold cufflinks, and a Hermès tie. His hair was parted on one side but this revealed no receding hairline or hints of grey. He had the appearance of someone who had been told by his mother that if you dress the part, you will get the part, but it was somehow all wrong.

'Allo, I am Julian Gross and welcome to this meeting,' he said. Dear me. As it turned out, Julian was on an internship while studying business at the local university and had just turned 23. 'I am going to do a hedge fund by myself one day,' he said in broken English.

After the initial five-minute chatter, I was about to break into our pitch, but Julian stopped me. 'I have a form,' he said. He pulled out a multi-page document and asked if we could 'stroll through it'. 'What is the name of your firm?' he asked. I wanted to say 'look at the fucking business card or your calendar!', but obliged.

'What is your address?' he continued. Jesus. He had simply printed out their due diligence form and was planning on filling it out during our meeting. Brian offered to fill out the information part of it while we talked investments, but Julian declined, saying the form was proprietary and he could not share it with us. We spent the next hour filling out his form, saying each sentence slowly so that he could write it down. We offered to fill it out ourselves twice more but he declined, saying it should have his tone. Not that his tone stopped Julian from asking us to formulate the answers. 'So I look good to my boss in case he reads it,' he said.

Back on the street, we felt empty and deflated. The road from the meeting with young Julian to a successful and thriving hedge fund seemed impossibly long. We would never in a million years have hired a guy like that for Holte Capital but here we were, selling our souls to him in the vain hope of an investment. I was furious with them for not taking us more seriously, but Brian reasoned that it was our own fault for taking any meeting that we were offered.

The first trip round Europe was a qualified success. Many of our meetings were in suburban or residential areas, and we would always allow plenty of time to get there, with the result that we often had time to kill in areas where there was no café, and nowhere salubrious to linger. On one occasion we found ourselves sharing a bus shelter with a bunch of local dope-smokers – a long way, we imagined, from the way George Soros went about recruiting investors. We did meet lots of investors who seemed to have a genuine interest and were considering investing with us. But we did not get anything near a firm commitment. A certain herd mentality seemed to apply: several were really interested but no one wanted to be first in. It was all very frustrating.

The next big leg of our road trip was our couple of weeks in the USA. Brian and I were both looking forward to this as we had both spent about a decade there between Boston and New York. I smiled when I first saw our schedule for the New York meetings. Our first meeting was with David Totti. Mr Totti had been a senior partner at Lazard Frères, although we didn't know each other. He was one of those people we minions knew to fear. He had since left Lazard and set up his own wealth-management firm next door.

Entering Mr Totti's lavish office, I thought I was in the movie *Wall Street*. Although I had heard of him terrorising associates, I had not imagined the mirror image of Gordon Gekko. At Lazard, he did not even deal with us analysts, who were one step too low for consideration, but left it to the associates, and I had therefore never met him. I felt as if he ought to launch into a tirade of abuse, calling me a useless piece of shit and how his two-year-old grandchild could do better financial models than me. You know. The usual stuff. He gave us the look of someone who had seen too many young Turks pass through his office, and asked me if I was friends with Felix Rohatyn and Steve Rattner. I told him that I obviously knew of them since their names were inscribed in analyst lore and Mr Rohatyn was rumoured to fire analysts who misspelled his name, but that they were too high in the hierarchy for me to know them personally. That it was a bit like asking a White House intern if she was friends with the president. OK – maybe that was a bad analogy. For a second I thought he smiled, but then he told us he only had 30 minutes, not the hour we had scheduled.

Although it was clearly a meeting that was not going to go well, I just loved being there. Not for a second would I swap his career with the one I will have, come rain or shine at Holte. I felt incredible pride at having struck out on my own and felt indignation rather than humility at his aloofness. He could not hurt me and I did not aspire to be him or anything like him anymore. Had I stayed at Lazard, I would probably have been a young vice-president who would still shit his pants when a name like Totti came up on the phone display. No fucking way. I would rather do dishes and live in a shed than live in fear of Mr Totti or someone like him, and have them give me the thumbs up or down at each annual review after dominating my life for the past year. Not happening. Not even if that life came with a guaranteed million-dollar cheque in January.

Not really in selling mode any more, but perhaps out to prove to myself that I was no longer a humble minion, I told Mr Totti that we were aiming to generate 10–12 per cent annual returns with limited market correlation. He held up his hand as if he was telling a classroom of unruly children to be quiet.

'This is really not that interesting to me – I can pretty much guarantee my investors 16–18 per cent uncorrelated return per year, and investing with you would only dilute those returns,' he said.

'Is that right?' I said defiantly. For the first time in the meeting, Mr Totti paid attention. 'If that guarantee is anything more than empty words or fraud, anyone would be crazy not to invest with you and you should be running the largest money-management firm in the world. I should tear up my presentation and market myself as someone who knows someone who can generate 16–18 per cent uncorrelated returns, which would be enough to make me an attractive prospect. In fact, you should take $100 and gear it five times and you would be almost guaranteed to double your money every year. Even the Ponzi schemes don't promise that!'

I assumed we would be thrown out of the office at this point, but Mr Totti was clearly having fun. He was almost relieved that someone had challenged him and we ended up spending two hours in his office discussing how much market correlation there is in many funds even if they go to great lengths to disguise it. When we finally got up, Mr Totti said he had enjoyed the meeting and would make sure that his firm gave us a close look. To his credit they did, even if they did not invest in the end. Perhaps they believed their own mantra a bit too much after all.

'That was an odd anti-sell,' Brian said, when we were back on the street.

'I don't know – there were a lot of old inner demons coming out in there,' I said.

'Well, perhaps one of those demons can get us a cab. We are already ten minutes late for the next meeting.' This meeting was on East 40th Street about ten blocks down and four over. We called ahead and said we would be running late and walked down Fifth Avenue as fast as we could without breaking into a sweat. Real managers don't sweat even when the kitchen gets hot. Getting to our destination 20 minutes late, we were stopped by the doorman. The man was clearly on his fifth doughnut and cup of coffee that day, and a small piece of sugar crust was stuck to his tie.

> Real managers don't sweat even when the kitchen gets hot.

'We're here to see Mr Hanson from Alpha Hedge.'

'Wrong address,' he said, without lifting his head from the sports pages. 'Been here ten years and nobody like that here,' he continued after we insisted that we were right. Shit. Not now.

'Fuck me. It was West 40th,' I said, realising my mistake. We covered the eight blocks across Fifth Avenue at full pelt and turned up 45 minutes late and sweating. There were already 12 people in the conference room when we entered. Most were courteous enough, if clearly annoyed at having to wait for us so long. On hearing that our New York schedule was full, two other investor firms nearby had come over to join the meeting at Alpha Hedge and could therefore not get on with their day until we had arrived. They had spent the past hour sitting around the table, checking their BlackBerries and drinking coffee. A couple of them were in their fifties and did not enjoy this apparent slight from two youngsters. We apologised profusely, but the meeting was already shot. A couple of minutes into my initial five-minute spiel, the lead guy from the host firm cleared his throat to indicate that he wanted the stage. He was elegantly dressed and somehow made the standard grey suit and white shirt look graceful. The rest of the room went quiet.

'So, Lars, you might be smart, but you have never managed a portfolio, and you, Brian, have never even worked at a hedge fund. Tell us again why we should give you money before you have proved yourself.' There was no hope, and within 20 minutes three of them excused themselves for other meetings.

One gentleman summarised his view of our strategies before getting up to leave: 'You eat like a bird and shit like a duck.' This was his way of saying that funds like Holte make a little bit of money a lot of the time and then lose it all in one big go. Not a great start to the day.

After New York, we went to Boston, Chicago and San Francisco. In true entrepreneurial fashion we stayed on friends' couches in most places and at our old Harvard final club in Boston. It was still easier to market in the USA than in Europe. Somehow it seemed that the US investors would like to invest in Europe with European national managers, but still felt comfortable with us as they knew and understood our US-centric background. They were more comfortable with a guy who had gone to Harvard and worked at Lazard than they would have been with an equally qualified European with less familiar names on his résumé. Probably half of the investors we saw in the USA refrained from the usual 'put us on your mailing list' and committed to visiting us in our London office, and perhaps two-thirds of those carried out their promises. This wasn't a bad hit rate, and made the trip worthwhile. We would soon understand how long would be the journey from initial and even follow-up meetings to an actual pre-launch investment. Nonetheless, having met us early and therefore known us over a longer period of time made it easier for some of these investors to give us money when we were in our post-launch steady-state mode.

5

Limping to launch

Getting to the starting line

After our big road trip, we had done plenty of promotion. Back in London, we had met most of the investors we intended to meet before our expected launch. We still had the follow-up process and plenty of second meetings lined up, but we were nervous. There were not many more meetings in which someone could pull a $10 million cheque out of his hat and save the day. It was now late August 2002 and, after a slight delay in our FSA application, we knew our launch was highly likely to be 1 November. Time to start closing deals and locking in capital. We were lucky that the leading European industry rag *Eurohedge* wanted to do an article on us. The ensuing half-page article praised us to the skies.

'Money can't buy that kind of marketing,' Marty told me.

Within a couple of days of returning from our road trip we had the first follow-up meeting in our offices. This was a US-based fund of funds that had explained to us how well we fit into their strategy and that they were ready to invest at launch. They were a bit coy about the amount, but said their minimum was typically $8–10 million. With nothing in the bank we would obviously take anything, but getting that much would be a fantastic boost. This was definitely an A-list prospect, if not our top one.

Partly to convey our cost-conscious nature, we rented one of the rooms in the basement of the building. There were three visitors, and after briefly introducing them to Massimo, we went downstairs. Mr Miller was the head guy and because we had met the two associates before and knew they wanted to go ahead with the investment, we knew he was the one to focus on. The meeting started well enough with me cracking my standard jokes.

'I am originally from Denmark . . . actually I am still from Denmark,' I would say, as if catching myself. I went on to describe to Pete, one of the associates, the intricacies of blending merger–arbitrage-type analysis with a more fundamental value approach. Pete clearly liked my explanation and nodded enthusiastically, apparently pleased that his recommended investment was showing promise in front of his boss. As he was about to make a follow-up comment to show that he understood what I was saying, he stopped mid-sentence with his mouth still open. Mr Miller was fast asleep and there was a bit of drool forming at the edge of his mouth. Poor Pete – this meeting was mostly about him showing his boss that he was able to find suitable investments and that he was clued-in enough to understand the strategy. I chuckled to myself. Pete slid slightly down his chair so he could reach across under the table and kick Mr Miller on the shin. Nothing. He had only kicked the briefcase.

Brian reacted swiftly. 'I forgot to bring the due diligence files down here – let me run upstairs and get them,' he jabbered, making enough noise to wake an elephant and startling Mr Miller awake.

'Where am I? And who are these people?' his expression clearly said.

We continued the meeting and I found myself modulating the tone of my voice to keep Mr Miller awake, almost yodelling my investor presentation at times.

'If these were not A-list investors, I would storm out of the meeting,' I mused inwardly, while knowing that actually I would have got up and sung like Britney Spears if that would have made them invest.

After another ten minutes, Mr Miller was asleep again. This time Pete was ready and kicked him, perhaps a little harder than he intended. Mr Miller jumped and gave Pete a death stare. I just kept talking as if nothing had happened and tried to look Mr Miller in the eye to keep him awake while slightly moving my head from side to side so his tired eyes would not be fixed on the same spot. And perhaps save him from further injuries to his legs. Alas, it was hopeless. We wrapped the meeting up fairly quickly as Pete said they had another meeting to get to. 'Oh, and please put us on your mailing list,' he said.

> After another ten minutes, Mr Miller was asleep again.

'Shit,' I thought, 'straight from A-list to mailing list...'

I caught up with Pete a couple of days later and he apologised. He explained that Mr Miller had slept really badly the night before after flying in from New York and admitted that he was not on top form during the Holte meeting. He had probably had 20–25 meetings with prospective funds that week and had heard similar things so many times so that he could no longer concentrate and would nod off.

'Wow, that makes me feel special!' I said.

'Well, don't take it personally,' said Pete. 'He liked what he heard and will be back in town in mid-December and would like to have a follow-up meeting then. I'll be sure to lace his doughnut with something to keep him awake.' With a November launch, December was much too late.

Other meetings became variations on the Miller theme, although no one actually fell asleep. There was a constant trickle of potential investors through our office – typically several per day – but none provided the breakthrough or firm commitment we needed. Although very few signed out and said definitely no thank you, nobody signed in with a 100 per cent commitment either. They all wanted to wait and see what other potential investors were doing. Lots of people seemed to genuinely like us and had no problem discussing future investments. But the same questions came up again and again: how much will you launch with, and will the fund be closed on launch? It was becoming clear that we were not going to launch the fund with enough money to close it to new investors, so there was no incentive for anyone to take the risk and invest early. Why not wait six months and get in when the show might be properly on the road?

We had to do something that would increase the appeal of a Day 1 investment without making us seem desperate in any way. The obvious answer was to lower the fees for early investors, but this had its own risks. Funds that lower fees are sometimes seen as inferior performers – almost like saying that we simply expect our gross (pre) fee performance to be worse than the competition. The other risk with offering lower fees is that it discounts the buzz of the money you raise early on. A fund that has raised $25 million with heavily discounted fees is less hot than one that managed to do the same at standard fees. But we had little choice and we decided to be very open and commercial about it. We would lower the fees to a level that reflected how much we needed the money. Early investors were badly needed and would get the highest discounts. As the asset size grew we would gradually lower the discount and start charging standard fees. Simple stuff really, but several people we casually asked about the structure unbelievably said that they had not heard something like it before.

We would not openly discuss the fee reduction with everyone, but quietly bring it up with investors we thought it could help sway. Those who were not going to invest at launch anyway would only think us more desperate for offering it to them, and we did not want the rumour to spread that Holte was desperate. We did not want to give discounts on our 1.5 per cent management fee, as that was our bread and butter, but we could reduce the incentive fee. We also came up with a multiplier so we had two factors to play with – the multiplier and the level of incentive fee. The Day 1 investment multiplier of 5× would mean that if you invested $1 million on Day 1, you would have the option to invest 5× (i.e. $5 million) at those same terms for the next year. Very appealing, we thought. The Day 1 investor incentive fee we decided on was 5 per cent rather than the standard 20 per cent incentive fee; if we made $100 return the incentive fee for that investor would only be $5 rather than the standard $20. The plan was to give those generous terms to the first $5 million invested, and then lower the multiple and increase the incentive fee as we got closer to our break-even level of assets under management.

Ignoring salaries, our break-even point was around $14 million in assets under management. At that figure, a 1.5 per cent management fee would yield enough yearly fees to pay for our office, Bloomberg terminal, computers, travel, and other expenses. This assumed no incentive fee, but since we could not assume that we would make money, we wanted to be conservative. If the fund ended up not launching I would also have been stuck paying large fund-related expenses such as Cayman registration, legal fees for writing a prospectus, etc., and I didn't want to contemplate this.

After our run-in with sleepy Mr Miller, I started to have my first panic attacks. We were now two months away from launch and still hadn't locked down any investors. Before we had approached potential prime brokers, I had estimated that my personal network alone would generate $10 million in assets. But I had failed to make any specific approaches. At the age of 30, most of my friends had yet to make their own money, but I still thought I knew a fair number of wealthy people. After the completion of our road trip I started to approach some of these. Although none were my closest friends, they were all people I knew quite well. I expected some of the natural scepticism that rich people often display towards 'friends' who ask for favours, but soon found that they had much more sophisticated ways of saying no. Nobody actually took offence or suggested that I was only friends with their money. On the contrary, they would try to help me by introducing me to either the main investment person at their family office (if they were very wealthy, with above say $100 million in assets) or, for the slightly less well-off, their private banker. Max Lichtenstein introduced me to LGT; one of the Rockefeller heirs introduced me to their fund, etc.

As I followed up with these professional advisers a common theme emerged. The advisers would often go out of their way to show that they already knew about Holte. It was just that they had decided that the investment did not fit their investment criteria for reasons that had nothing to do with Holte, but rather to do with the brilliant investment strategy they had planned for the family. This way, they were able to head off any further discussion about Holte, or any suggestion that they might be rejecting us on our merits – either of which might have caused friction with their client who had made the introduction. At the end of our marketing efforts we scraped together about $1.25 million from our private network of friends.

Working the percentages

Once it had become clear that our personal networks of potential investors would not ensure a successful launch, we refocused on the institutional investors. I had more than 200 meetings with about 100 investors over a four-month period. After hearing 'We don't invest on Day 1, but good luck and keep us on your mailing list,' again and again and again, I found it increasingly hard to get fired up for each meeting.

We kept a working sheet on which we tried to calculate the weighted amount of money we expected for our November launch. We divided potential investors into four categories from A to D, with the D-list being the ultra-long shots. We also had a 'personal contacts' list. We would estimate how much each investor would invest if they were to invest, and then assign a probability to the investment. So on the A-list we had five or six investors we thought were 25 per cent likely to invest $3–4 million and three or four investors who might invest more – say $7–10 million – but were perhaps a bit less likely. At the lower end, we might have an investor we reckoned 10 per cent likely to invest $2 million – so we would add a weighted amount of $200,000 to our expected assets under management. At the end of this process, we had about 70 names on the list, and estimated that we would raise about $25 million.

A launch asset base of $25 million was about half what we had hoped for when we started, but it was still a reasonable sum and probably meant we could pay ourselves modest salaries. I was reassured by the fact that a friend in New York had gone through the same exercise before the launch of his hedge fund a few months earlier and eventually launched within a couple of million of his $45 million estimate. Our calculations were sound enough in themselves, but they took no account of the cascade effect of failing to attract that first substantial investor. Once one potential investor has dropped out, the odds against every other investor lengthen – so that although we might reasonably assess investor A as having a 20 per cent chance of investing $3 million, this percentage chance would fall dramatically once investor A was aware that investors B, C, D and E had not invested.

Meltdown

With a couple of weeks to launch, we began calling our 'hot prospects' and casually asking if we might expect an investment from them. Then we called all our second-tier prospects, and soon pretty much anyone we had talked to. Often this was the fourth or fifth time we had called or emailed these people, but one can't be too proud when one is walking the plank. The answers were depressingly similar in their coded language:

'We haven't yet talked about it in the investment committee.'
(Meaning: Don't blame me!)

'Our lawyers are still going over the prospectus and may not get to it in time.'
(I am looking at more interesting funds I might actually invest with.)

'We just need to see how you get on in the early days.'
(We don't want to be the only jokers to give you money!)

'We really want to give you money, but we already have so much exposure to European managers.'
(No chance!)

Without a single investor, we were getting desperate. We could blame the herd mentality but that didn't make us feel any better. The only money we could be sure of would be my own limited capital. I had planned to divide my assets so that I could fund the operating loss at Holte Capital until the firm broke even (I allowed 18 months and assumed we would raise at least $5 million), have some money to cover living expenses, and finally some money to put in the fund. The third pool was clearly important as it was the amount I could be certain would actually be invested on Day 1, but at $250,000 it would not have been enough to persuade Morgan to let us launch the fund.

Every morning I would come into the office with high hopes that there would be an overnight email from the USA or Asia with the breakthrough investment, only to be disappointed. I began to think about the circumstances in which I would have to admit defeat. I began to imagine that people were laughing at me. I fantasised about being marked for life with a tattoo on my forehead that read 'hedge-fund failure'. I thought about

> I fantasised about being marked for life with a tattoo on my forehead that read 'hedge-fund failure'.

opting to become a salary man somewhere. I could not concentrate on anything. I would stare at my screen and repeatedly ask Brian to walk round Berkeley Square with me to discuss our situation and what desperate measure we could come up with to save the situation. We would circle the square so many times that we had to switch to nearby Grosvenor Square for more rounds so people would not think we were the local drug dealers.

We had gambled on not needing a seed deal, and it seemed the gamble had failed. I might be the 100 per cent shareholder of Holte Capital, but by mid-October 2002 this looked like 100 per cent of nothing. At our peak of self-confidence – some would say arrogance – we had broken off conversations about a $30 million investment from one party that wanted 15–20 per cent of revenues for four years for their investment. Now we would have bitten off the same hand extending that offer. We discussed going back on the whole project and starting the seed conversations again, but if the past five months had proved anything, it was how hard it is to raise money. And not being able to raise money makes you a far less attractive investment for a potential seed investor. Besides, this would be a six-month process that we just did not have the stomach for. So we kept going towards our starting line of 1 November.

With one week to go, we finally made a breakthrough. A private investor we knew via a friend subscribed for $500,000. The administrator promptly sent him a notice saying he was investor number 001 – just in case he was not already aware that he had invested in an amateur outfit. We told our administrator to make the next investor number 052 and then go up from there.

'How many more are you expecting?' she replied. We were so on edge at this stage that we would take offence at any real or perceived slight. 'We have a contract with you that we expect you to honour!' we bellowed into the phone. She clearly had no idea that she had said anything wrong, but meekly agreed and apologised. Perhaps we were not the first hedge-fund managers she had seen with frazzled nerves.

'Am I having a nervous breakdown?' I would ask myself on my daily wanderings around Mayfair. Not that I really knew what a nervous breakdown felt like. With just days left before launch, every hour that went by without anyone investing brought us closer to the abyss. Every time a ping on the computer signified a new email, I hoped it would bring the relief I craved – but it never did.

I was inside the Starbucks at Piccadilly when Brian called on the mobile. 'We got a million dollars. You are soooo money, baby!'

Not exactly. But now we knew we would get past the $2 million we considered the absolute minimum to get started. We would be limping across the starting line, but it was as if the wind changed direction and was suddenly behind us. I almost ran back to the office with new-found energy to start on work I had previously left in my 'to do' pile. The pile should really have been called 'to do if you have a business'. Someone had actually trusted us with a million dollars! They could have invested that money in anything in the world, and they had chosen to give it to us. We could not let them down. We really shouldn't have been so proud, but I was ecstatic. I sent a text to Puk that we had to celebrate with a bottle of cheap wine. It seemed somehow appropriate.

Absurdly, the one-million-dollar investment was from a young guy who was running a small private fund of funds for rich folks in Monaco and was under the impression that one of the giant funds of funds we had been talking to would also be investing. This was not in fact the case, and if our young friend had known that, he certainly would not have invested either. He later told us as much.

We raised the grand total of $3.55 million and by any standard were well on our way to becoming a start-up failure. Another fund we knew which also launched on 1 November had more than double the assets we did on Day 1 yet decided to call it quits in under two months. On the day before our launch, a junior person from Morgan Stanley took us for a pint at the local pub to say good luck and well done. He kept talking about how tough the environment was at that moment, but left us with a sense that Morgan had clearly expected us to raise more money to start with. I was reminded of my mother saying, 'I am not angry, just disappointed'.

The following day on our way to the Underground after work, Brian and I walked past Claridges where we could see the patrons at Gordon Ramsay's restaurant. As we joked what a large part of our new assets under management it would cost to eat in there, we saw the Morgan prime-brokerage team taking another start-up out to dinner at one of the private rooms. I think I saw a magnum of champagne in the middle of the table, but quickly turned away to avoid eye contact with one of the people we recognised in the room. I guess there are hedge funds, and then there are hedge funds who don't get invited to the big boys' parties.

The stress surrounding our launch was made far worse by my lack of perspective. Businesses fail to get off the ground every day and often the entrepreneurs are stronger for having tried. I still had a lovely fiancée, a great group of family and friends, my health, and a strong résumé in the bag to get my career back on track, yet I had fallen into a mindset in which failure was the end of the world, and nothing else mattered. It had certainly been a soul-destroying eight months, and my ego was badly bruised, but on 1 November 2002 we arrived at the starting line and launched Holte Capital.

PART TWO

Becoming the real deal

6

Mickey Mouse fund

Starting out

Holte Capital opened for business on 1 November 2002. We arrived at the office drained from the drama of the previous week's fund-raising. At the 8am opening bell Brian sent me an email: 'Houston, we have lift-off', which led to more self-deprecating banter about what a big bad hedge fund we were, now that we had $3.5 million to throw around. 'Corporate Europe, be afraid – Holte Capital is ready to make you dance', 'The evil empire is ready to strike', etc. Then it was back to work.

In the run-up to launch we had put together a 'paper portfolio' of securities we planned to invest in once we were in business. The only thing we needed to do was to scale the size of each security for the total assets of the fund. Had we launched with $50 million, a 1 per cent position would equal a $500,000 investment and, assuming a $100 share price, that would mean we had to buy 5,000 shares. As things were, we would only have to buy 350 shares.

Within a couple of hours on our first day we were ready to make our first trade. The $50,000 buy order would be placed through Richard at JP Morgan, a broker I had talked to since my first days at HBK. After the usual banter about how honoured he would be to execute our first trade, I explained that we would like to buy 620 shares in the Belgian company GBL, working max. 20 per cent of volume at a max. price of 85 euros per share. Massimo and Brian were listening in.

'Hang on,' said Richard, before asking, after a pause: 'You do know this is only about a 50 grand order, right?'

'Yeah, I know. Starting small,' I said.

There was another pause. Then Richard asked: 'Lars – how did fund-raising go?'

'It was pretty tough going to be honest. We launched with a little under $5 million.'

'That is tough,' he said, 'but I gotta tell you that if this is going to be your typical order size, you might want to take your trades elsewhere. I don't mind helping you at all, but if the higher-ups see these sizes consistently from Holte they might ask me to cut you off from research and stuff.'

'That's cool,' I said. 'Thanks for letting me know.' But he had certainly taken the wind out of my sails.

Although we were a lot smaller than we had hoped, it felt great to be in business. Lots of people have endless cocktail-party conversations about how they plan to start a hedge fund, but we had actually *done* it. This was our baby and we were going to try our hardest to make it work. After months of talking about what we planned to do once the fund launched, we were now doing it – analysing companies and industries and coming up with clever hedging strategies that could express the nugget of value we thought we had found in each trade. This was what running a hedge fund was meant to be like, and it felt great. Of course, it would have felt better with more money in the bank, but once we were fully absorbed in the analysis, our dire financial state seemed to matter less. The first week was spent putting together the portfolio we had planned before launch. After that first reality check with Richard we began to do a lot of the trades using the cheap and electronic direct market-access platforms that Morgan Stanley had provided us with. That way, we avoided humiliating reminders from brokers about how small our orders were.

But our first few days were rough. By the end of the first week we had lost money every single day. By the end of our second week we had lost money in nine out of our first ten trading days. I left the office that Friday evening in a state of puzzled dismay. What was going on? Was there something systematic in the portfolio that meant that we were somehow

> This was what running a hedge fund was meant to be like, and it felt great.

destined to lose money all the time? I spent the weekend poring over the trades and thinking about what might be behind the string of losses, but failed to come up with anything. After this rough beginning things somehow stabilised. My heart rate came down a bit and results began to improve. By the end of our first month we had recovered sufficiently to end with a small positive return. Or 'up small' as we would tell our small group of investors.

I was writing our inaugural monthly investor letter when Brian came to me with the final net returns for the first month of business. They were quite a bit lower than I had imagined.

'It's the expenses that are killing us,' he said after I queried the figures. 'The monthly expenses for everything are about 17 grand and on top of that you have the performance and management fees.' We had talked about the effects of fees and charges on our returns but we hadn't worried about them because we hadn't thought we would be starting with so little capital. Now we had reason to worry, and the table below shows why.

Gross return	0.71% *(after trading costs)*
Expenses	0.48% *(17K over $3.55 million in assets)*
Management fee	0.13% *(1.5% over 12 months)*
Incentive fee	0.02% *(20% of remaining profit)*
Net return	0.08%

The expense structure for a hedge fund hit a small fund like ours disproportionately. Since many of the charges such as legal set-up, listing fees, administrative fees, clearing fees, etc. are fairly fixed, the investors in a small fund take a larger part of the financial burden than if they had been invested in a large fund. Some charges, such as stock-loan fees, funding charges etc. go up with the size of the fund, but those were not what concerned us. If an investor lost 3–4 per cent per year in expenses by investing with Holte Capital relative to investing in a larger fund that made our fund-raising argument to potential investors harder, and meant that even with the cashflows from fees with around $14 million in assets under management we would fail to break even. In order to avoid putting our investors at a cost disadvantage compared with a larger fund, I decided to personally pay for all the fund expenses as a result of the fund being smaller than $50 million in size. While this meant we could market the fund on more equal terms with larger funds, it meant it was costing me personally $17,000 a month. On top of the monthly operating losses from costs such as office, equipment, and salary for Massimo, Holte Capital was becoming an expensive affair for me.

Mickey Mouse moments

For every hedge-fund manager with as little capital as Holte had in the early days, there are going to be moments when you realise just how far you are from the big time. These were some of ours.

Million, not billion

An old acquaintance called Paul got in touch soon after we launched Holte Capital. He had heard through friends about my impressive fund and was keen to introduce me to a very wealthy Middle Eastern client of his over a drink in a couple of days.

'I don't know about impressive,' I said.

'Ah. Always underselling,' he replied.

I shrugged and planned to meet them. I arrived at the grand lounge of the Dorchester Hotel on Park Lane in Mayfair just after 6pm and they were already drinking champagne. Paul introduced me to Mr Ali, a guy in his mid-20s whose appearance suggested someone more at ease in an expensive nightclub than in a conference room. There was no title on his business card, yet I made the fair assumption that it would not have said 'assistant' if there had been one. The young Mr Ali felt no compulsion to say what he did or who he represented. He did not even invite us to use his first name, but remained the aloof Mr Ali for the short duration of our acquaintance. Soon it would not matter anyway.

After chatting casually about the party scene in Miami vs Cannes and finding me a bit boring and stiff for their liking, Paul got to the point.

'Well, Joe told me about your great success. Congratulations. Outstanding,' he started. Then turning to Ali, he said: 'Lars here is a friend of Joe's from New York. He went to Harvard and is now running a $5 billion hedge fund here in London. You guys should look at it,' he said.

'Interesting,' Mr Ali said. 'What do you guys focus on?'

Wait a minute, I thought. Did he say $5 billion?

'Er . . . I think you have a few too many digits there. We are only at about $5 million in assets, not billions . . . I wish!' I said with a nervous laugh.

▶

Paul looked at me with a blank expression. Mr Ali gave him a look that said: 'Why are you wasting my time with this joker? There are night-clubs to be attended to.' Nobody said anything – clearly there was no point in my going into the finer details of our investment strategy. Finally Mr Ali took charge. 'Well, there was obviously a misunderstanding. Five million dollars is just too little for us to look at, but perhaps you can get in touch if you grow larger. Say ten times larger?' he said without a hint of irony, before running upstairs to change for dinner, hotly pursued by an embarrassed Paul.

I was left alone with a humbled ego and a bill for £45 for two glasses of champagne and a glass of house red wine.

'Can we borrow one share?'

One of our early trades involved taking a long position on an investment company with diversified financial interests, which included some shares in Berkshire Hathaway, the company run by investment guru Warren Buffett. To get the most accurate hedge, we found ourselves in the odd position of having to sell short his share. Because of the high price of a Berkshire share (around $50,000), we only needed to short one share to be accu-rately hedged, and even that was slightly more than we wanted to be short. As a matter of course I called up the Morgan Stanley stock-loan desk.

'Hi Stacey, it's Lars. Any issue with borrowing Berkshire Hathaway stock?'

'No,' she said. 'It looks pretty easy. How many are you looking to borrow?'

'Just one,' I said, already feeling stupid.

'One? One thousand?'

'Nope. Just one little share. Don't worry – we'll sell it carefully,' I said, laughing at my own 'small-timeness'.

'OK then . . . One full share coming your way,' she said, and hur-ried off the phone so she could share this great story with her colleagues. Somebody actually wanted to sell short one Berkshire Hathaway share!

'Thanks,' I said, cursing Warren Buffett for not having done a share split that would have allowed me to borrow one thousand shares at $50 instead of one share at $50,000. Who borrows one share anyway? Apparently Holte Capital does . . .

Getting the currencies right

In the months after the Holte Capital launch I was defensive about our poor showing in the asset-gathering game. If we were asked how much money we managed, we would say: 'We don't really disclose that.' Or: 'Some of our investors prefer us to keep that confidential.' One investor had mentioned in passing that it would be a good idea to keep our assets under management (AUM) confidential, so the line was sort of true. This was harder among friends who did not expect us to keep such things private. But asking how much money I managed was a bit like asking my annual income – and later I would watch many people do the mental arithmetic after asking our AUM, performance, and confirming that I owned the business.

I was at dinner with Puk and some Danish friends of hers who were visiting London. The husband worked in equity sales for a small regional Danish bank and knew enough about hedge funds to ask the right questions. Clearly he had heard from his wife how Puk was now engaged to this hotshot London hedge-fund manager and was genuinely interested.

'What kind of strategy do you invest in?' he asked. I did the brief version to avoid putting our dining companions to sleep. The dreaded 'how much do you manage?' followed.

'We are around 30 million,' I replied, giving the amount in Danish kroner making it sound eight times higher than it actually was, immediately thinking to myself, 'Please don't ask the currency'.

'Is that dollars or pounds?'

'Oh, I thought you meant Danish kroner,' I volunteered, with my vain exaggeration exposed. His look said quite clearly: 'Am I missing something or is that a really small amount?'

Puk came to my rescue and moved the conversation on to more important things like the Harrods sale. I was left feeling terrible. It is one thing to fail while giving it your best shot. It is far worse to lie to make yourself look better, and fail even at that.

7

Breaking through

Getting traction

The problem in the months after launching the fund was that there was nowhere to hide. After the usual pleasantries, people just kept asking about our AUM. When we had to answer '$3.55 million' or more vaguely 'just under $5 million', there would inevitably be a silent pause, tinged with incredulity.

We tried lame excuses like, 'We just wanted to start with a small amount of money from friends and family to get our systems going before taking in larger institutional investors', but nobody would buy that one. Besides, it was a lie. So I stopped pretending.

The truth was that we had tried all the ways we could to get assets and failed. It was embarrassing, and when people tried to be sympathetic, it often made it worse. 'It's tough out there,' people would say. Or: 'I heard of XYZ fund that raised less than that and is still around.' Or: 'Don't worry – once you've been around for six months, people will take another look at you.'

> The truth was that we had tried all the ways we could to get assets and failed. It was embarrassing.

This last comment was certainly true, but it didn't feel like it two months after launch. We soon realised there was no point in trying to lure major investors into the fund if we were only running $3.55 million. Barring a seed deal, a regular investor in the fund wouldn't want to represent more than 30–40 per cent of the fund's total assets, so we were looking for investors of $1–1.5 million, not $8–10 million. We also re-approached a couple of the seed investors, but our launch timing worked against us. Potential seed investors now had all the evidence they needed that we were unlikely to raise a lot of money in the near term – a key measure-ment in a prospective investment. They would ask us to revert in six to nine months when we had built a bit of a track record and were 'on a more stable footing'. Add to that a six-month period of due diligence and negotiations, and we would be dead before getting a seed investor. There was no point.

I was getting quite depressed about the whole situation. There seemed to be little evidence that we were going to be able to attract the investors we needed. Our returns were fine in a very tough market, but we were far too small for anyone to notice. The folks at Morgan Stanley suggested hiring another analyst to make us look more credible, but I was worried about the extra expense. Also, who would want to join a $3.5 million hedge fund as the fourth person? One evening in early December after Brian had left for the day, Massimo asked if I would be a business-school reference for him for entrance next fall.

'Let's face it,' he said. 'Holte Capital might not be around in September.'

It was not an unreasonable request. One afternoon after another, prospective investors were deciding not to invest in Holte Capital. Puk sug-gested we postpone our planned May wedding. 'No way,' I insisted. 'I'm not going to let this take over my whole life.' As if it hadn't already done so.

That evening on my way home from work I stopped to buy flowers for Puk to reinforce my commitment to our wedding. I was standing by the cash register with my 'reduced to clear' bouquet when Borut, a friend from college, saw me.

'No wonder you get all the girls,' he laughed.

The race to find investors for $1–2 million meant hitting up the smaller funds of funds and family offices we had met while fund-raising and paying them special attention that many of them were not used to. When an investor with a potential investment of $1–2 million approaches a multi-billion-dollar hedge fund they might get a meeting with marketing person number six, but the George Soros equivalent is unlikely to find time in his schedule. At Holte Capital they would get all the love and attention they could desire.

Three months after launch, nobody was going to think Holte Capital a substantially different prospect from what we had been in the months before launch, except that we had not raised any additional capital. But there was a key difference to our post-launch marketing meetings. Once a potential investor had made a decision to take a meeting at Holte Capital they could immediately invest. Instead of giving us throwaway excuses like, 'We will revisit after you launch' or 'We want to see the systems working', now they knew where we stood. We were tiny, but we were in business, the systems were working, and we were making money. And those who came to see us were aware of that. At the end of each meeting we could ask potential investors if they planned to invest the following month, and we weren't embarrassed to do so.

There were a couple of small funds-of-funds investors who were interested. They each had about $100 million under management. Because we were so small, they could have a small to medium-sized investment with us, yet have access to management (me) that they would be denied elsewhere. They would have liked us to be larger, but they liked our early fee rebates. Also, the fact that I was committed to covering the expenses meant that the investors were not at a cost disadvantage versus investing in a larger fund.

In February, three months after our launch, we made a mini-breakthrough. A Chicago-based fund of funds decided to invest $2 million and committed to investing another $1 million the following month if there also were other investors investing more. They liked what we did and that our initial returns had no market correlation. The $2 million meant we could keep going at least another couple of months. The following month we built on the momentum. A UK fund invested $2.5 million, a Kuwaiti family office invested $1 million, and a New York-based fund of funds invested $750,000. With these new investments, our new friends from Chicago kept their commitment and invested a further $1 million. Excellent. From being a $3.5 million hedge fund on 31 January, 2003 we went to work on the morning of 1 March running a hedge fund of around $11 million. Not quite a big-time hedge fund, but fast getting towards the break-even point where we could cover our expenses.

Being headhunted

One afternoon, as I was reading through a research report, the phone jolted me to attention.

'Holte,' I said with the urgency of an execution trader.

'Lars Kroijer?' demanded a woman with a perfect Margaret Thatcher accent. 'Hi, this is Susan Wilson. I run a top-end recruiting firm here in London and I was given your name by several sources in the industry as a potential candidate.'

'Aha. You do know I run my own fund these days, right?' I asked.

'Sure, but a couple of the guys said you might still be open to this specific position I am trying to fill. One said that things have not worked out quite as well as you had expected and the job I am talking about involves running the London office for a top US fund. Big money and your own fund! I am going to be in the West End tomorrow. Perhaps we could have a quick coffee?'

I said I didn't think I would be interested, but I would be happy to have a coffee after the markets closed.

The following day, 15 minutes early, the receptionist told me Ms Wilson was waiting for me. Turning up during the closing auctions? Clearly not a market person, I thought.

She was looking annoyed when I came to pick her up right after the market closed. At around six foot tall with satin hair and understated jewellery, she clearly wasn't used to being kept waiting, even if she had turned up early. 'You look younger than I thought,' she said, with a disapproving look at my casual outfit.

'It's the makeup,' I joked, without drawing the faintest of smiles.

I suggested Starbucks, but she turned her nose up at that, and we agreed on a Japanese teahouse nearby. As we walked the 300 yards to the teahouse I noticed a Jaguar trailing us slowly.

'My driver,' she said, as if that was the most natural thing.

'Here's the deal,' she said as soon as we sat down. 'You get your own fund inside their set-up. You are guaranteed to be running $250 million in the first year, but they plan to double that and you will take in outside money after six months. Until you are running $500 million, you will be on a minimum package of $1 million per year with an expected additional bonus. After that you get 40 per cent of the economics to be shared with your team.'

I did some quick numbers in my head. This really was quite attractive.

'Why me?' I asked.

'Well, this is not a job offer,' she said. 'They are interested in you and three other guys. One of the head guys met you on your road trip to New

York and was impressed. When he heard of the tough start you had had, he thought you would be better suited with some real institutional backing. Besides, how much fun can it be to run $11.7 million?'

I was impressed that she knew our up-to-the-minute assets under management, but simultaneously annoyed because her comment suggested that my whole situation and prospects could be summed up in one number: $11.7 million.

I told her there might have been a point in my darkest hour when I would have jumped at this kind of opportunity. As things were now, there was no way. Holte Capital might not be a home run, but it was my show and I felt like a genuine entrepreneur. We had cre-ated something together, and going to manage money for someone else was going to feel like a step back – whatever the size of the salary. The meeting was a good reminder of how happy I was to have taken the step to start Holte Capital.

> Holte Capital was my show and I felt like a genuine entrepreneur.

I gave her a couple of names of people who I thought would suit the role and we started to walk back towards Berkeley Square. About 20 feet down the road the Jaguar caught up with us and Susan jumped in before the driver could rush round the car to open the door for her. Several weeks later, I received a note thanking me for my help and saying that one of the guys I had mentioned to her had taken the job. She probably got a $250,000 recruitment fee for her troubles.

Our big breakthrough

We had grown massively in percentage terms in the previous months, but after five months and at $11–12 million in assets under management, Holte Capital was still a small fund that cost me money to run every month. Momentum was important and we were having many conversations with potential investors to keep increasing our assets. Our sales pitch was made a lot easier by the fact that there were now clearly a number of investors who had overcome their res-ervations about our size and decided to invest in Holte. There was still a long way to go, but at least each investor could feel better in the knowledge that they were not alone in partnering with Holte Capital.

Smith Capital Partners was one of the largest funds of funds in the world. They had been chatting with us on and off since four months after I had quit my former job, but we had still put them in the 5 per cent investment probability at launch. Post-launch, they came back for another meeting. Soon afterwards, they asked for a third meeting, this time with one of their more senior people from New York. Then we had another meeting with their due-diligence team to assess our operational competence. Although the operational side of the business was in perfect order, Brian always worried before these meetings. People would hardly ever decide to invest on the basis of an operational due-diligence meeting, but they might well decide not to. We had naturally assumed that Smith was doing the footwork in case our assets grew to a size where they could seriously consider their minimum investment of around $20 million – they wouldn't want to account for more than a third of the total assets in any fund.

Then one afternoon in March I received the kind of call dreams are made of. It was Quintin from Smith Capital Partners – our main contact there, and someone I would later be a business school reference for.

'Are you sitting down?' he asked after the usual pleasantries. 'We are probably going to invest $25 million for next month.'

I was caught completely off guard and before I could formulate an adequately casual response I blurted out: 'Are you shitting me? For real?'

I could see Brian and Massimo raise their heads in unison. Quintin laughed on the other end of the phone – he knew how important this was to us, and relished being the bearer of good news.

'For real,' he said, before going on to discuss the necessary steps involved – the investment committee meeting, the reference checks and so on. Then he revealed that Smith would almost certainly be looking to invest another $25 million over the next several months if others also invested more. He just wanted some sort of note or letter from me saying that nobody would get better terms than them, and assuring them that we had the capacity to invest up to $75 million over the next 12 months.

I could hardly believe my ears. This could be the making of Holte Capital. We would give them anything they wanted and they were not asking for much. Quintin told me why they were thinking of coming in with such a large amount so early in the fund's life.

'You guys are great,' he said. 'We think you might in time become one of the large funds and we hope that by coming in with a lot of money early on when it still makes a big difference to you we will create the foundations for a strong long-term relationship on top of getting good returns.'

'Foundations for a strong relationship?' I spluttered. 'I would give you my sister in marriage if you asked me right now.'

Brian and Massimo had long stopped what they were doing and when I hung up the phone we started celebrating.

'Are you ready for the big time, Bud Fox?' Brian asked me, quoting from the film *Wall Street.*

'Born ready and raring to go!' I quoted back.

Fearing premature exuberance, we discussed the things that could still prevent an investment from Smith and they largely had to do with system or reference due diligence. From the outside it was hard to tell if Quintin would call us when the investment was 'somewhat likely', 'very likely', or pretty much 'money in the bank'. We naturally hoped for the best, but still felt a residue of doubt nagging away at us. We would not know for sure until another three tortuous weeks had passed and the money was finally deposited.

In the days leading up to the investment committee meeting at Smith Capital we prayed the phone would not ring. In the past we had hoped the phone would ring or emails come with messages of potential capital. Now we felt that the absence of contact from Quintin meant there were no hiccups or need for more information. Of course we knew the tranquility would not last.

Quintin called. 'We've hit a snag,' he said. My heart sank. Then, after a pause . . .

'I'm just joking. It went through investment committee. Should hit the accounts around month end.'

'You just aged me ten years,' I said with a sigh of relief, giving a thumbs-up to Brian and Massimo.

I was at a lunch meeting with a company management at Merrill's offices when Brian sent me an SMS: 'Smith money arrived. All good.' I closed my eyes and quietly said 'thank you' to nobody in particular. The money had arrived, and Holte Capital had arrived.

That evening we went to The Guinea, our local pub down the street from our office, in what had become the typically understated Holte way. Although the day's events clearly called for champagne, we preferred to opt for plenty of our respective alcoholic favourites. My relief was beyond

> My relief was beyond measure. After almost a year of turmoil and a continued series of rejections and letdowns we were on the up in a big way.

measure. After almost a year of turmoil and a continued series of rejections and letdowns we were on the up in a big way. On top of the $25 million from Smith, another couple of investors had invested smaller amounts and we now had around $40 million in assets under management. We were well past cashflow break-even point and had a growth profile we could be proud of. With the new capital, we would be able to afford good salaries and still have lots of money left over to expand the business. This did not even take into account the fact that we hoped to get a nice fee at the end of the year for our share of the profits. I was already doing the numbers in my head but soon gave up – arithmetic and lager don't mix. We were still a long way from being a big or even a medium-sized hedge fund, but that evening we felt like champions of the world.

8

Scaling up and meeting the Godfather

Scaling up

The large inflow of capital came with its own set of problems. Practically speaking, Holte Capital, like most hedge funds, accepted subscriptions on a monthly basis. So with this very large subscription, we were basically managing $15 million on the 31st of the month, then managing $40 million when we turned up for work the following morning. With more capital, we went from having bought very few securities to a position where we had to put $25 million into the market over a couple of days.

A larger amount of money did not mean that we were going to invest in different trades, but that we would buy more of the securities we already had in the portfolio. We would scale up in each security so that each dollar invested with Holte Capital represented the same security mix as before the large capital inflow. The brokers obviously liked the larger orders as it meant they received larger commissions. We had spent months explaining to them how we were just starting out and would soon be making bigger orders and knew this argument would only work for so long before they cut back their services, so it was nice to be fulfilling our promises. Although we only had $40 million under management and were not yet even a medium-sized fund, we were certainly less puny than before and could show real growth. These larger orders allowed me to bend the ear of an Italian broker who set up a series of meetings with portfolio companies in Milan.

In the world of hedge-fund investing in complex corporate structures, it is impossible to ignore Italy. The country has a history of cross-ownerships, family-controlled holding companies, litigation, and share-class arbitrage – all things that provide fertile ground for hedge-fund managers. At the top of this spaghetti tangle of influence is the old investment bank, Mediobanca. Nothing in Italian finance gets done without Mediobanca being involved. At the time, the bank held a large number of stakes in prominent Italian businesses, including the insurance company Generali. Mediobanca in turn was owned by a larger group of leading Italian companies joined at the hip by a shareholders' pact never to sell their stakes to outsiders, effectively blocking a takeover of the company and furthering the bank's image as a tool which the élite use to control Italy. The previous chairman of the bank, Enrico Cuccia, was a legendary figure whose reputation was only enhanced after his remains were stolen from his grave. All very mysterious!

With new management and changes in the previously opaque accounting system, funds like ours could more easily work out what the non-holding part of the bank consisted of. In the past this would have been a futile exercise. Mediobanca's remaining core business was the main invest-ment bank, but also included smaller business units like brokerage and asset management. Although it was by no means simple, we could try to esti-mate the value of these businesses using conventional valuation metrics like price/earnings, price/book value, etc. Once we had separated the actual business units from the general stock holdings, we could estimate how the overall value compared to the current stock value:

A brief explanation of stub trades and holding company discounts

If Mediobanca's quoted holdings post-tax were valued at 9 euros in a 10-euro stock, the market was essentially saying that the rest of the bank-ing businesses were valued at 1 euro. This is what a typical stub, or rump, trade looks like. You say that the stub is trading at 1 (this can easily be a negative number and often is). An alternative way of looking at this is to take your estimated value of the remaining businesses and add them to the value of the holdings (9 in this example) and come up with a total net asset value or NAV (this analysis ignores the minor complications of debt). If you say the businesses are valued at 6 then the total value is 15 (9 + 6) and the company is trading at a 33 per cent discount to its NAV (5/15). This is what is meant by a holding company discount.

Stub calculation		Discount to NAV calculation (%)	
MB market value	10	MB public holdings	9
MB public holdings	9	MB core business	6
Stub	1	Total value	15
		MB market value	10
		Discount	*33*

Applying this analysis in the market you would then be able to create a trade where you go long Mediobanca (10 euros) and hedge 9 euros-worth of its holdings proportional to their value to recreate the stub trade through quoted market securities. So if 25 per cent of the value of Mediobanca's holdings were its stake in Generali, 25 per cent (or just over 2 of the 9 euros) of your hedge should be Generali. To make the trade genuinely market-neutral (or at least money-neutral) you would then have to hedge the residual exposure of 1 euro with something like the Italian market or comparable banks. In cases where the stub represents such a small part of the market value (1/10 in this case) you would typically not hedge it or hedge the components relative to their share of the net asset value of 15. So you would hedge 60 per cent of your position (9/15 or 6 euros) with Mediobanca's holdings and the remaining 40 per cent (6/15 or 4 euros) would be a hedge for the core business.

There are a million iterations of this kind of trade, and hedge funds love them.

Our planned trade in Mediobanca was fairly simple. We believed that the stub was trading too cheaply. Like many Italian companies that are involved in a myriad of cross-holdings, Mediobanca historically traded at a large discount to the sum of its parts. In the years before our trade, the discount was approximately 40–45 per cent, depending on how generously you valued the core business.

Meeting the Godfather

The Mediobanca headquarters is near Milan's famous La Scala opera house in the centre of town. I walked up a quiet street and mused how appropriate it was that this secretive Italian banking powerhouse was hidden in an anonymous office building behind the artistic landmark.

The inner sanctum was very quiet and did not seem like the kind of place that saw lots of loud noise, but rather where leaders of industry and politics could sneak in and out without being noticed. I was greeted by a young woman from Investor Relations who seemed slightly nervous and insisted on holding doors open for me.

'Mr Manzini from Banca Intesa suggested we make someone senior available to you and Mr Nagel would like to have a brief meeting followed by lunch.'

'That would be fine,' I said casually while I digested her words.

Mr Nagel was chairman and CEO of Mediobanca and a very big cheese. A really, really big cheese. Why on earth did he want to meet me? What on earth did the Intesa guys say to get me this meeting? Of course I played it cool, as if this was the kind of meeting a company of Holte Capital's standing would naturally expect to get.

I was completely taken aback when I met Mr Nagel. I had expected a mix between Don Corleone and Silvio Berlusconi, complete with heavy accent and an entourage of goons. Instead, a smiling young man greeted me like an old friend saying, 'Mr Kroijer? Am I pronouncing that right? You must be Swedish?' He laughed when I told him that not too long ago people could be killed for mistaking a Dane for a Swede. 'Wait; did I just make a joke about murder to someone who 30 seconds ago I thought might be the Godfather?' This guy was good; nobody ever makes me feel that comfortable that quickly. He led me into our lunch room from the adjacent meeting room, suggesting we eat while we talk. Later I thought about how my stupid preconceived notions of what people were like would make me a worse investor and made a note to myself to keep an open mind. Mr Nagel looked to be around 40, but perhaps because he was so obviously at ease in these impressive surroundings he seemed older. Or maybe just wiser.

'So you are the next hotshot hedge-fund manager?' he said as we finally sat down. I was puzzled. Six months ago I thought my world would collapse before Holte's launch. Now the leader of perhaps Italy's most powerful bank was calling me a hotshot to my face. And he didn't even seem to be joking! I figured that in a meeting like this it made no sense to try to bullshit. Someone like Mr Nagel would probably see right through the awkwardness of someone who is not telling the whole story and would quickly write that person off as a waste of time. Also, I felt that by being open and frank I would stand a better chance at having the treatment reciprocated and learn more as a result. Besides, it is a lot easier to be open and frank about being a $50 million fund which is growing quickly than being a $3.5 million fund that hopes to take on more assets in the future.

Perhaps it was just the unfailing charm of a seasoned investment banker, whose skills at putting people at ease would have to surpass those of a priest on death row, but Mr Nagel seemed genuinely interested. He kept asking about how I had gone about starting Holte and seemed to enjoy my various anecdotes of skirting failure before we launched. He was surprisingly interested in our trading strategies too. With a background in M&A (mergers and acqusitions) work he was quite knowledgeable about merger arbitrage and had a fair number of useful comments. Almost half an hour into the meeting, I was still doing most of the talking and he was happy just to sit back and hear my perspective on things. I found it quite flattering that a person like this felt he had something to learn from me.

Traditionally hedge funds have been coy about their trading strategies, often because they felt their proprietary analysis and technique gave them their edge. In this meeting I took completely the opposite approach. I explained in great detail the thinking behind our Mediobanca trade and how we hedged the trade to make it market- and sector-neutral. Mr Nagel listened with interest when I told him how we shorted the stocks in his portfolio.

I used the following analogy. Suppose, for simplicity's sake, you assume that Mediobanca consists of only three parts: its stake in Generali, a stake in Telecom Italia (in reality there were over 25 stakes), and the core banking business. If you buy a share in Mediobanca you are effectively saying that you have a view on at least four things that are all hard to work out:

1 You implicitly claim to know whether Generali and Telecom Italia will go up or down in value (and if you know this for sure, why not just buy Generali or Telecom Italia?)

2 You also claim to know whether the value of Mediobanca's core banking business (investment banking, brokerage, asset management, etc.) will do better or worse than its domestic competitors and how domestic finance will fare generally.

3 You claim to know whether the Italian market will go up or down and therefore effectively take a view on the Italian economy (since these three business units are likely to move up or down with the market).

4 Finally you claim to know whether the holding company discount at which Mediobanca trades will increase or decrease.

That is a lot of stuff to know to be successful! By contrast, Holte Capital took a view on just two things. We thought that the holding company discount at which Mediobanca was trading would eventually decrease, as the new management seemed intent on being more open. We also took the view that the core banking business would not perform worse than its Italian banking peers, and kept a close eye on any available market data to prove this. This meant we had much less to know, even if our trade looked much more complicated than simply buying a Mediobanca share.

Mr Nagel seemed to like our thinking, even if he could not encourage us to short the Generali stock. He offered a few technical improvements to our analysis, changing the book value of some holdings (relevant for capital gains taxation if Mediobanca was to sell a stake and incur taxes) and making a couple of comments about our method of tracking the value of the core business. There was an issue of some rights connected to the stake Mediobanca had in Ferrari, but that was a minor correction which, oddly, confirmed that there were no larger issues. He made the perceptive comment that it was obviously much easier for him to like and agree with our analysis since I wanted to be long on his stock rather than short. In general, walking through the analysis seemed to confirm that we were not completely off-base in our work on Mediobanca. You could argue that our trade was actually a form of flattery for Mr Nagel. We were aiming to eliminate every part of the business except the core business which he managed directly, and we were betting on his ability to narrow the holding company discount. Above all, I took from the meeting what I had hoped: the feeling that there was a real desire to reduce the discount at which Mediobanca was trading relative to its fair value. And if anyone could actually do something about that, it was Mr Nagel.

Back on the streets among Milan's well-dressed financial circles I felt excited. About our trade. About our prospects. About how quickly we could go from taking dozens of hopeless meetings with potential investors to long lunches with titans of industry.

There was no doubt in my mind that my meeting at Mediobanca was successful because I was well prepared and shared with Mr Nagel an angle of analysis he probably had not seen ten times that day already. It was probably refreshing and he may even have gotten something out of our time together. A couple of months later I was in a similar meeting with the CEO of SAS (the airline) and remember being embarrassed at my own ignorance about the company. I asked about that company's plans for a stake that they had sold years earlier, and generally found I knew far too little about the stock to ask interesting questions or make use of the answers. Rather than continuing the meeting I found a reason to excuse myself so I would not take more time from someone who was busy trying to save thousands of jobs (he soon gave up trying). Later I called the broker who had arranged the meeting to apologise for being so unprepared.

The real deal

Spending money and being happy

With the Smith investment, we had passed our cashflow break-even assets under management to become a profitable business. We charged our management fee every month so the impact was immediate and we would now receive a further $30,000 per month in fees alone. Since nothing had really changed in our little firm and we had incurred no extra costs, this money went straight to the bottom line. At last we were able to have an internal meeting to decide how to spend our new-found wealth. 'Salaries would be a welcome change!' suggested Brian. It was hard to disagree.

In the months that followed, we saw for the first time the positive side of having significant momentum. We received an average of $10 million a month in new assets under management both from our new large investor, but also from investors who were now comfortable that there was little risk in investing with Holte. The floodgates had not quite opened, but being less desperate for money clearly made us a more attractive prospect. What a new and nice change it was to sit in meetings with potential investors who were looking for reasons to invest, rather than for reasons to stay away. Without keeping track we felt that a meeting in our office had gone from being 2 per cent likely to generate a new investor to more like 10–15 per cent. And that made me more excited about taking meetings. Rather than the dull faces of people trying to fill their schedules that pervaded earlier meetings, the potential investors were now engaged and interested, suggesting that they were actually seriously considering an investment.

So we discussed how we might spend some of our new wealth to improve our performance. Massimo and I shared a Bloomberg terminal – would we be more productive if we had one each? Brian would be able to monitor some trades and thus reduce my time doing that if he had a terminal too. Should we add Reuters as another news source? Should we buy laptops so we could be more productive when away from the office? Should we hire another analyst or more support for Brian? An IT person? Paid lunches brought to our desks? There was no shortage of suggestions of ways to spend money, but I was keen to make a personal profit.

This early period of growth was a very happy time for me. Leaving my old job and launching Holte Capital had caused some emotional strain, and the consequent stream of rejections had left me feeling utterly drained. My self-esteem had plummeted. But now at last I felt vindicated. Our performance was fine – we were up just under one per cent per month and rarely lost money. Crucially, our return profile showed minimal correlation with the markets – essential if you claim to be market-neutral. I suspected that our risk levels in the fund were far too low, but felt that the last thing we needed was more risk just when things were starting to look good. On my morning walk through Hyde Park to our offices, spring 2003 felt like a suitable metaphor for the blossoming of Holte Capital. One morning I even found to my surprise that the crazy old lady who made bird sounds near Lancaster Gate smiled back at me and nodded. My positive change of mood must have been contagious.

In May 2003 Puk and I got married in a lovely ceremony just north of Copenhagen near where we both grew up. The setting was straight out of a fairytale with the old white stone church surrounded on three sides by spring-green birch trees and a cemetery leading down to a quiet lake. And, yes, it was about two miles from the town of Holte. Our children would later be baptised in the same church.

I had already spent the vast majority of my adult life outside Denmark, either in the USA or England, so coming home for a big celebration felt like being lifted out of the fray to observe my life from above. I was happy and excited to be doing something that I so firmly believed in, and felt lucky that fortune had smiled on me. Many of the speeches at the reception in the nearby hunting club touched on the themes of being true to your beliefs, love and commitment, finding meaning in it all; but our guests didn't forget the traditional poking fun at the newlyweds! It only struck me years later that I had failed to notice the obvious analogy between my blossoming and happy private life and the recent happy state of my new firm.

After a five-day honeymoon in Spain, it was back to work. Puk still reckons I owe her about three weeks' worth of honeymoon.

With assets comes glitter

We were still under a year old when we passed $100 million in AUM in the fall of 2003. There was no wild celebration. We did not even realise it until late in the afternoon on the last day of the month. Brian received an email from an administrator saying that there would be another $6.5 million invested from a certain sub-account for the following month, with no explanations. The money simply arrived after the email and that was it. We were on a list of approved investments for the sub-fund of one of our investors and when they received additional capital from their investors, some would automatically be allocated to Holte Capital. What we would have given to be on a list like that at launch.

> We were still under a year old when we passed $100 million in AUM in the fall of 2003.

We quickly found that what mattered was not just our level of assets, but the momentum we had along with it. Once we had gone from $50 million to $100 million in four or five months and from $3.55 million to $100 million in less than a year, some people seemed to think we were capable of anything. We used this momentum to remedy some of the worst terms our various counterparties had imposed on us when we had no negotiating power. Gone were the $100 per trade settlement fee, the 100 bps (basis points, i.e. 100 hundredths of a per cent) funding spread, and the minimum IT spend. Our average brokerage commission went from around 15 bps per trade to something like 8 bps. The ease with which we could bring this down only served to remind us how hard it had been in the early days, when we were not only preoccupied with raising money, but also being slowly bled dry by counterparties who wanted their pound of flesh early in case we didn't survive.

Despite this dramatic surge in our fortunes, I was amazed to get a call from someone at *Eurohedge* who told me that we were being considered as a nominee for 'Start-up of the Year' at their annual awards. Our returns had been quite good, but nothing spectacular. We were up about 8 per cent after fees for the first 10 months of the year. Our returns had shown very little volatility but, rather, had been steady over the year and shown little correlation with a choppy market during the same period. I thought it strange that with hundreds of hedge funds in London alone, this was enough to stand out. As it turned out, one of the criteria for the award was to have had average annual assets of over $100 million. Since we had spent our first couple of months averaging only about $5 million, we were nowhere near, so we didn't qualify after all, and the next year we would no longer be considered a start-up.

I still went to the awards dinner and had a good time. For a crowd that is so often depicted as leeches on society and borderline criminals, I found it ironic that the venue should have been the halls of the Royal Court of Justice. I couldn't help musing on the possibility that some of the people attending in their pin-striped business suits might one day end up wearing a striped prison uniform instead. But no one felt the least bit self-conscious. On the contrary, like myself at Holte Capital, all these managers clearly saw themselves as providing a very valuable product to their investors, and their presence at the dinner seemed to validate this. Although many of them were getting paid a lot to do something they loved, they saw any sugges-tion of crime or wrong-doing as uninformed or misguided. At this point in 2003/4 the hedge-fund industry was growing in leaps and bounds and those who had been running funds for a while felt that their track record of creating value was beyond reproach.

At the dinner there was a strong sense of self-congratulation in the air. I was there as a guest of one of the banks that paid for the festivities by buying tables for their clients. After trying to tell people that I was nearly nominated for start-up of the year and being given a look that said 'yeah, right', I decided there was no point in trying to be a big hitter. The short acknowledgement speeches from the winners of various sub-categories were predictable and boring. A couple of guys got drunk and started insulting long-only managers as being the idiots who provided opportunities for us brilliant hedge-fund managers, but mainly speeches covered the usual 'thanking the team' stuff. I was probably just jealous that I didn't get to go home with a prize.

10

Being corporate

Paying people

After we passed $100 million in assets under management in the fall of 2003, spring of 2004 quickly took us above $200 million before levelling off just under $300 million. We were not doing anything new or better. In the eyes of potential investors, however, we were no longer a risky start-up fund, but instead a growth story with a stable, if boring, return profile. Around this time, the hedge-fund industry was seeing massive new investment in general and a big part of our growth was undoubtedly down to some of our investors looking for places to put their new capital. Not that we minded. In the space of 18 months we had gone from a no-hope start-up to become a decent-sized hedge fund with a promising outlook where everyone was paid well. How quickly things can change.

> In the eyes of potential investors, however, we were no longer a risky start-up fund, but instead a growth story with a stable, if boring, return profile.

We all relished getting salaries. What a concept: you actually get paid to work! Our framework agreement on relative compensation meant we could avoid the awkward conversations that often cause great friction in small start-up companies. We had agreed that the three of us would make the same amount of money until we all made £250,000 per year. Once the firm reached a size where the three of us could make that amount and still have more money to go round, we would re-evaluate things. As I owned 100 per cent of the business, it was easy for me to say that 'we' would decide what happened next, but Brian knew I would not take advantage of this. The mutual trust that came with our long friendship had helped cement our business relationship. I had wanted this compensation agreement to avoid precisely the destructive friction that sharing equity ownership can create in the early stages of a firm when there is already too much uncertainty. Unfortunately my fears of frequent divorces in the hedge-fund industry were proven correct eight months after launch.

It had been clear for a while that the personal dynamic between Massimo on one side and Brian and me on the other was not working. It was perhaps somewhat unfair to judge this sort of thing during a period of such stress and hardship, but constant bickering had rendered the office environment unpleasant for all of us. We knew that Massimo had an opportunity to attend Insead for business school that would expire when classes started in September. As a result we made the difficult but probably mature decision to part ways over the summer. Typically for the hedge-fund industry, none of our investors took much notice. Brian and I had a replacement lined up weeks in advance in the form of Alberto Lage from Spain, who stayed at Holte Capital to the end. To the investors this was just another personnel change. It was a strange feeling that something so important to us, losing one-third of our team, mattered so little to the outside world: another symptom of the insular world of the hedge fund.

In all my time working in hedge funds I still don't think anyone has come up with the optimal solution to ownership and compensation structures, if indeed such a thing even exists. It later had massive benefits to me to own 100 per cent of the business, but, like all owners, I felt that the firm could not exist without me and that I paid those who worked for me fairly – I don't think I ever had anyone leave because they were dissatisfied with their compensation.

Expanding the team

'Everybody wants to join a hedge fund these days; finding someone will be easy', people used to tell me when I talked of difficulties with recruiting to match our growing assets. The eagerness people had to join the industry often reminded me of the Internet revolution I had experienced at HBS in 1998. At times it seemed as if everyone who had worked at any finance-related firm wanted to get into hedge funds.

The financial allure of hedge funds was obvious. There were any number of magazine articles about star managers and how much money they made and how young they were – probably true for the most part. The seriously big money in private equity funds or investment banking typically meant being a slave to the existing partnership for the better part of a decade. In comparison, a young superstar at a hedge fund could start making big money after only two or three years of outstanding performance. If the desired bonuses failed to materialise, there would be other funds willing to give you a better deal, or perhaps even some financial backers to help you set up your own fund. All this by the time the guy has hit 28 (I say 'guy' because unfortunately there are very few women running funds or working at them). In hedge funds, the rapid growth a firm may experience from the consistently stellar performance of a young manager can easily justify giving a substantial stake in the business to that person. The smaller share of a much larger pie will be more valuable to the other partners.

Apart from the promise of large bonuses, many people were attracted to the dynamic and meritocratic environment. Here, nobody cared about who you were or how old you were, but only about the quality of your ideas and their ability to make money consistently. At Holte Capital we could theoretically look at any investment in any area as long as it was in line with what we told our investors and it made us money. 'We can bet on horses as long as we find a way to win and remember to tell our investors,' I would joke with potential employees. I always waited for the rumour mill to start and a concerned investor to call up and ask, 'I hear you've started taking Holte's money down to the bookies, is that true?' but it never happened.

With more assets under management by early 2005, we added Zach and Oliver to our team of analysts and Sarah as a trader. In a year and a half, our three-man team had doubled in size and, when we added Doriana as our office manager, Holte started looking like a real office. Before the four of them joined the team, things still felt like a couple of guys sitting in a room. Now we were a real hedge fund, with our phones ringing and a constant stream of meetings in the office, even if our fairly academic approach to investing kept the atmosphere peaceful. We even had a company pub for post-work pints on a quiet street off Berkeley Square.

As the hedge-fund industry grew massively during 2005 and 2006 towards its peak in 2007/2008, a clear trend emerged. There were more and more people with hedge-fund experience interviewing for the positions we offered. This made sense. When I first interviewed for a hedge-fund position in early 1998 there were not that many hedge funds around; I doubt that someone with my background today could end up meeting an industry giant like Richard Perry at their first interview. Back then, not having hedge-fund experience was no real barrier to getting a job in the industry simply because so few people did. Later on, the number of hedge funds exploded to nearly 10,000 and many funds had already been through a period of contraction or closed down so there were many more candidates who had experience working at hedge funds.

We tried several routes to find new people. We would post jobs on Bloomberg and in financial newspapers, email our entire business network including brokers and investors, and ask friends. Typically we would receive 175–200 résumés for a job. Brian would have the dubious pleasure of going through all the résumés and deciding who to interview. Sometimes I would hear him chuckle on reading a particularly amusing application. One guy was unfortunate enough to have been at Enron's energy trading department after spending three years doing audit work at Arthur Andersen in Houston. Another was a self-taught prison inmate whose success in the online virtual stock market competition had inspired him to go clean and join a hedge fund (is that going clean?). At the other end of the spectrum we received some résumés from some truly world-class candidates, for whom Holte was an alternative to setting up their own fund. Two people I interviewed now run large hedge funds.

A lesson I quickly learned when interviewing people was to make my expectations clear early in the process. Although most people we talked to were well aware of what was expected of them and what they could expect in return, some candidates seemed to think that joining a hedge fund was like winning the lottery. After spending an hour interviewing one candidate for a $75,000 job with a likely bonus of another $75,000, I asked about his compensation expectations.

'Well, I am obviously not set on a number as I have to perform first,' he said, 'but I imagine a total package of around $1.5 million would be in order.'

He seemed insulted when I told him what I wanted to pay him.

By the time Brian had gone through the many résumés and had an initial conversation, I would typically take over to discuss specific trade examples and explore the candidate's thinking on investments, before passing them on to Alberto for an analytical grilling. But Alberto felt we were spending too much time with candidates who lacked the basic necessary analytical skills, so I devised ten simple questions that I would ask everyone we interviewed for an analytical position. Here are five of them (and if you want to work in a hedge fund, it would be useful for you to work out the answers):

1 When you try to separate out the stake Company A owns in listed Company B, what role does minority interest on the balance sheet of Company A play in finding the deconsolidated financial statements?

2 French company Renault has a large stake in Japanese Nissan. Discuss currency exposures and what you could do to limit them. Suppose Renault guaranteed Nissan's debt: how would you think about the magnitude of this potential liability?

3 A company changes depreciation of an asset from 10 to 12 years. What will this mean to its stated cash flows and earnings? What does it mean to cash flow and earnings if you change AR (accounts receivable) days from 25 to 35 next year?

4 Company A has a large unfunded pension liability. Is this a real liability? Should it be counted as debt? If you know that the net deficit is $10 million do you care about gross assets and liabilities? What else do you want to find out?

5 What is 'duration' in the context of bonds? Does a bond have beta exposure to a market?

I found many of those I interviewed unable to answer the questions to the level we required, however nice they were as people.

Frustrated by his inability to answer the questions, one guy shot back at me: 'What do you make in a year?' (My only answer was a confused expression.) 'Well, whatever it is, hiring me would double it. I don't give a shit about fancy finance formulas; I am here to make money!'

Since we were in the business of making money by whatever legal and ethical means we could, I asked him to elaborate. 'Well, I just know if markets are going to go up or down. I can feel it in my gut. It's that simple!'

He seemed offended when I somewhat snobbishly suggested the paradox that someone who knew which way markets were going to go was interviewing for a job at a fund and not already richer than Warren Buffett, but accepted our difference of opinion that people can consistently predict the direction of the stock markets. For all I know, he may be well on his way to being a billionaire today.

Myopia

The myopic nature of hedge-fund asset flows made long-term operational planning a challenge. Did you really want to be stuck with a ten-year lease on your office if all your assets and fees could be gone in six months? How about promising an end-of-year bonus to lure a great candidate from a highly paid job when you had no idea of the size of the bonus pool at the end of the year? It was not easy. But, like all entrepreneurs, we played the hand we were dealt, and adapted. I would frequently get letters in January from students in business school who were interested in joining Holte Capital the following August and think to myself, 'August? By August we could be three times bigger or completely bust! August is a million years from now!' as I pondered the 15 changes in our P&L (profits and loss) on my screen in the time it took me to think that.

The human side of constantly being evaluated on short-term perform-ance numbers was a drain. Within months of launching the fund I came to recognise how much impact the publishing of our monthly numbers and investor letter had. As we toiled away each day, trying to come up with new trades or make money from existing ones, any existing or potential investor would invariably ask, 'How are you doing this month?' or 'How was last month?' The investors obviously had the right to know – it was their money after all – but I came to hate it. It was as if the performance number provided a neat summary of all your work and aspirations, and there was no need to say anything else; you were summed up in one number. A good friend of mine who ran a small fund described it like this:

> *'You are a number. Basically if you have bad performance numbers you are a bad person . . . If you have high assets under management and are therefore rich, you might get a reprieve, but only for so long . . . If you are small and perform poorly you think everyone from your mother-in-law to*

> **The human side of constantly being evaluated on short-term performance numbers was a drain.**

the postman is giving you a pitying look saying, "This is clearly a guy out of his depth", and you begin to be defensive and see humiliating ridicule in innocent comments from those around you. If you are at a dinner party and a friend at Goldman tells you he has been promoted, you take this to mean "At least I know what I'm doing." One month I was down 4 per cent in an up market and I thought everyone was looking at me thinking "How can anyone be so stupid?" It is not a happy place to be.'

While I didn't feel the pressure of monthly returns quite as keenly as my friend, running a market-neutral fund did exacerbate the pressure to perform. Since your fund was meant to be uncorrelated to the market, a bad run could not be put down to tough markets. We were meant to make money every month and provide investors with assurance that not all their investments would do badly at the same time. Whenever we performed poorly in bad markets we thus had the double failing of doing poorly but also failing to provide our investors with the protection they had counted on us for. If you had a bad month while other hedge funds did well, you generally felt crap about yourself; and it was a whole month before you could send out an investor letter with a new number. With the weight of a bad monthly return hanging over you, the pressure to shine was even greater.

11

Activist investor

The no-BS rule

If there was one thing I always enjoyed about small financial shops like Holte Capital, it was the complete absence of internal politics. Compared with Lazard Frères, where even 22-year-old analysts like me quickly learned they had to navigate the office minefield to find the best deals to work on, my hedge-fund experience was simple. If we found meetings a waste of time, we would stop having them. If wearing suits with colourful bow-ties or matching pink hats would bring success, we would happily wear them. We were there to make money for our investors and, as long as we didn't break any laws, nobody cared how we went about our day. I would read articles or books about how the heads of the large investment banks often represented the cream of office politics rather than brilliant financial analysts, and chuckled at how appropriately this described my time at Lazard.

Because of the analytical nature of our work the office atmosphere at Holte was not unlike that at a library or research institute. Our work revolved around painstaking analysis of often-convoluted businesses, tearing apart opaque financial statements and finding ways to hedge out the exposures we did not like. This was not a place where traders would scream 'Dump the sucker!' or 'This baby is going to 100!' followed by the obligatory 'Yeehaw!' The situations we looked at did not involve revolutionary changes in technology or medicine – we just did not think we were as well-equipped as the competition to claim an edge in these trades – so there were few Silicon Valley or McKinsey buzzwords in the office. Instead, you might hear something like: 'Once you adjust for the decline in the currency-adjusted bond values of the already under-funded pension plan . . .'

Since our trades were hedged on an individual basis, this also allowed me to escape the dull and thankless prospect of giving friends and family stock tips. People would ask, 'What should I buy?' and be frustrated with the response: 'Well, if you buy $10 of A and hedge $3 of B and $6 of C and use gearing to double your long and short exposure, you have a great trade.' Soon people stopped asking and I could avoid the embarrassment of either losing money for friends or having to continuously feed people asking for more stock tips if the recommendations worked out. After five years of running Holte Capital, my mother would still ask me if markets were going up or down and then proceed to ignore me when I told her that my fund actually tried to avoid caring about that by making returns that did not depend on the markets. She would sceptically say, 'I know. I know. But does that mean you think the markets are going down?'

What I called the 'no-bullshit rule' obviously also applied to our trades. Each trade on our portfolio had to pass these often-repeated tests:

1 The alternative to this trade is cash, which in certain markets is a great investment (assuming the bank you save with does not go bust, of course!).

2 When you come to work each morning, you are effectively buying the portfolio again. If you started today with cash and no securities, is this really the portfolio you would create?

3 Are you guilty of positive affirmation in your trades – i.e., are you looking for reasons why your trade is good rather than why it can go wrong?

4 Do you really have an edge on this trade?

Finding trades and not spreading too thin

As our assets continued to grow, so did our investments in the securities we held. We had broken down the portfolio into a number of what we rather pretentiously called 'trade theses'. A trade thesis was a trade idea or hypothesis that was individually hedged to be market-neutral. We thought this had the advantage that we would hedge each trade as was most appropriate for that specific idea. Doing it our way we felt that we would be better able to avoid the dreaded mid-cap/large-cap bias where you are long mid-cap names and hedge those with the wider market through a large-cap-dominated index – a very typical bias for hedge funds. But we also avoided the industry bias that can come from being long on a particular industry and short on the whole market, which in turn may be dominated by different industrial sectors.

One trap we were keen to avoid was the need to keep changing the scope of situations we looked at. At $3.55 million in AUM, virtually any public security is liquid enough that you can invest in it. But if you had invested in a security where, for whatever reason, your maximum investment size was $500,000, you would have a problem once your fund grew to more than $50 million in size – particularly if your fund was geared so that your gross investment size was larger. If you continued to invest in smaller illiquid situations you could either increase the number of positions in your portfolio to a level where your knowledge in each situation was diluted, or you could look at new positions as the fund grew. Early on we tried to avoid this by only looking at situations that we could also be invested in if the fund grew larger than $100 million. After reaching that size, we would have to hire new analysts to find more trade situations to look at as we did not want to be in a situation where each analyst (including myself) was looking at so many trade situations that they would not have enough time to learn everything about all of them. We felt that the scope of situations in our investment mandate was broad enough that we could keep doing the same type of investments (with some natural evolution over time) until we had approximately $500 million invested. As things turned out, it was only really after we reached $600–700 million that we started to see liquidity problems in the Holte portfolio.

Once Zach, Oliver, Sarah and Doriana had joined the team, we found that we spoke nearly all the languages in Western Europe between us. We would scour local newspapers to see if there were interesting angles of attack for local trades. One day, I came across a small article in *Dagens Industry* – a not-too-serious Swedish business newspaper that seemed to prefer writing about rich entrepreneurs than about actual business. The article referred to Gothenburg-based company Bure and discussed how the company was in trouble after a share-price decline from 30 Sek (Swedish Krona) to about 3 Sek and that the company needed to restructure and planned to raise money through a rights issue. A rights issue can take many forms, but often it involves a publicly listed company seeking to raise money from its shareholders by giving them the 'right' to invest more money in the company at a discount on the prevailing share price. So a company that trades at $10 may give a right to buy one more share at $7 for every five shares you own in the company. It is a tactic sometimes used by companies in trouble (and thus unable to get a loan) and Bure was certainly in trouble.

Bure and the corporate raider

Bure was still hung-over from the happy Internet days of half a decade ago. The company had a large number of stakes in smaller technology-related businesses as well as more substantial stakes in a couple of quoted businesses, a healthcare company, a private equity fund, and a large Nordic infrastructure engineering business. It had some debt but nothing that seem likely to cause bankruptcy in the short term, although there had been a very close call a couple of weeks earlier. Not surprisingly, there had recently been a change in management from a high-flyer to a more pragmatic industry person from the auto sector.

A couple of things made Bure attractive to us. There was no controlling shareholder who could stand in the way of the new management's economic decisions. Also, for whatever silly reason, the rights issue was terribly complex and likely to scare away a large segment of retail investors, many of whom were undoubtedly already sick of the Bure stock and much poorer because of it. Because Bure had so many bad associations, it was also likely that brand-name Swedish investment companies would shy away from having Bure appear in their holdings. The rights issue was structured as follows: for every share you held in the company you would be given one new share, two warrants with a five-year exercise period and a strike price of Sek 0.75, and a zero coupon bond with a par value of Sek 2.50 that would mature five years after issue (zero coupon bonds don't pay interest but trade at a discount to the eventual payment that reflects the time to maturity and credit risk). Jesus, it was confusing. After the recent mess, who would understand that, much less want to invest in it?

After spending a couple of weeks analysing Bure, we came to the view that the company was trading at about a 45 per cent discount to the net asset value. Although high, this discount level is not unusual for a European holding company, particularly when the values in the non-quoted businesses are not transparent and there is turmoil in the organisation. Two things about Bure intrigued us. The new and convoluted capital structure left shareholders confused and we felt there was a good chance that one of these three instruments (share, warrant, or zero-coupon bond) would be severely mispriced. Also, we felt that the new management were open and willing to acknowledge that nothing was sacred in trying to turn the business round. I asked if this included the possibility that the organisation might be worth more if it

> all the components of a good trade were present: an incorrect valuation, a potential catalyst (large restructuring), and a willingness in the management team to listen to reasonable suggestions from investors.

ceased to exist and they replied, 'Theoretically, yes'. Then again, without a dominant shareholder to support management, a shareholder-friendly attitude was clearly the order of the day. So we felt that all the components of a good trade were present: an incorrect valuation, a potential catalyst (large restructuring), and a willingness in the management team to listen to reasonable suggestions from investors.

When I met the senior management in Gothenburg, they explained to me how hard it had been to raise money and that there had been a point when they were 48 hours from declaring bankruptcy before they secured financing. They were certain that there was real value in Bure's holdings but there had simply not been enough cash around to meet its obligations. Now that funding was secure, they were understandably keen to avoid staring into that abyss ever again. Boy, did that sound familiar.

Once we felt comfortable that the valuation was correct, we started to build a position in Bure. We mainly bought the warrants and bonds. There seemed no point in buying the shares when we could get the same exposure more cheaply through the warrants and, now the company had enough cash for the foreseeable future, the bonds seemed to have a generous yield and low bankruptcy risk. When we had acquired a 5 per cent stake in the company (through the warrants), we had to declare to the stock exchange that we were a significant holder. That felt cool. Little Holte Capital was a significant shareholder in a company that was a borderline Swedish household name.

It was amazing how different our worlds were. The CEO of Bure, Lennart Svantesson, was a real hands-on guy who relished and excelled at sorting out operational issues facing the portfolio companies. His struggles involved meeting delivery dates and managing working capital while facing down the unions. He even used the term 'just-in-time delivery' which was the first time I had heard the expression since business school. By contrast, he clearly did not know what to make of me. At 33, I was too young to have come up through the ranks of an operating business to suddenly appear on his list of leading shareholders. He knew that I ran my own investment firm and therefore he did not have to look over my shoulder to see who was really making the decisions, but he also gathered that I had not grown up with wealth. In the circumstances, I was impressed how quickly he brushed aside any reservations about my lack of pedigree in order to listen to my ideas for the company.

Nonetheless, to Lennart and many others with an industrial background, there was something odd about a system that allowed someone like me with no industry experience to find himself in effective control of a company like Bure that employs thousands of people with families and mortgages. And there I was, a guy in his early thirties telling experienced company management what to buy and sell, who to hire and fire, and having the power to back up those demands with action.

What we wanted was simple. The company needed to reduce its overheads as much as possible. It was bloated, and future investment was unlikely as long as Bure's shares were so cheap. The company should then look to reduce or sell its stakes to raise more cash, although with the new financing, this was less urgent. The cash should then be used to buy back warrants and bonds while maintaining a conservative gearing level. To encourage management, we tried to incentivise them with options, but were politely told that this was not the done thing. To Lennart's credit, he listened to my arguments and his main objection was to the idea of selling companies that were just beginning to turn around before he had had time to correct things. At one point in the meeting he even said: 'So you don't even think I should sit here? Should I be next door buying warrants?'

I enjoyed reading comments on the Internet after we announced our material holdings in Bure. There was some speculation that we were an evil asset-stripping London hedge fund which was, oddly, not too far from the truth – except for the evil bit, of course. One guy had found out I was president of my Harvard final club and thought this meant Harvard was somehow involved. My favourite was someone who thought we were probably part of the British football club Aston Villa because one of the ends at Villa Park stadium is called the Holte End.

As part of our attempt to convey our message to Bure's board of directors, we got in touch with the other major shareholders in the company. Generally speaking, they agreed with us and some had even tried similar things with management themselves in the past. One investor was the Swedish pension system, AP Fondet, that had their own reasonable disagreement with being part of a group that could be seen to be shaking up a Swedish company, but they were also not going to be an obstacle. When I met them, it was clear that we were all on the same page.

Slowly, things started to happen; never as quickly as we would have liked, but it was steady progress nonetheless. The overheads were reduced and smaller stakes were eliminated. Bure started to walk the walk and a new chairman was elected. This was real progress. The company stopped talking about new investments and started looking at its own capital structure as somewhere to create value. Shares and warrants were repurchased and eventually the bonds were bought back. The share rallied to the point where it no longer traded at a discount to its holdings and our job was done. We exited Bure when the stock was still trading about 15 per cent cheap. I remember thinking, 'That was really good fun' and that I had enjoyed the work.

What made Bure fun was the fact that we felt that we had taken on a highly complex situation and actually made a difference. Rather than being along for the ride of a rising stock we felt we were part of making that rise happen. It is a wildly overused term but we felt that we *had* helped to create value for the Bure share- and bondholders. That we made good money along the way was obviously the main selfish objective but the feeling that we had actively helped make this happen gave a great sense of meaning to what we do.

Corporate finance summary

For those with an interest in corporate finance, here is a brief explanation of why Bure's actions were likely to enhance shareholder value and why we could profit from them.

Soon after the shares, warrants and bonds were issued it was obvious that there was a lot for us to do. The bonds traded at a very high yield to maturity, and the warrants traded below their intrinsic value (i.e., you could buy a warrant, exercise it, and pay less than the share price – this should not theoretically happen, but the exercise process took about two or three weeks).

We thought it was the warrants that provided the best opportunity for management to create value. Imagine the scenario where a company has an equity value of 100 (divided over 100 shares each worth 1.00), but a NAV (net asset value) of 150. The company would trade at a 33 per cent discount to NAV. Suppose now the company sold 25 worth of assets and used the proceeds to buy back its shares at 1.00 per share. Pro forma for this the company would have a NAV of 125 and a new equity value of 75. Unless the shares traded up in price the discount would have gone from 33 per cent to 40 per cent (50/125). To maintain the discount of 33 per cent to NAV the share price would have to increase to 1.11.

Starting NAV		Pro forma NAV	Discount Adjusts	Price Adjusts
Net asset value	150.0	Net asset value	125.0	125.0
Shares outstanding	100.0	Shares outstanding	75.0	75.0
Price per share	1.00	Price per share	1.00	1.11
Market value	100.0	Market value	75.0	83.3
Discount	33%	*Discount*	40%	33%

In reality the shares would probably have traded up more as management would have signalled to the market a willingness to do something about the high discount the share was trading at.

Any manager of a holding company in Europe is well aware of this, if only because a plethora of hedge funds remind them daily. Where Bure was different was that there were more warrants than shares outstanding and with the same amount of money they could buy back three times the number of warrants, making the impact on the discount to NAV far more dramatic. Similarly, you could argue that the company was borrow-

▶

ing money at high interest rates to own assets that were valued at a large discount the minute Bure owned them (namely the holding company discount). Selling some of those assets to buy back some bonds would have the double impact of reducing the discount to the gross asset value, and also reducing the future risk of bankruptcy when the bonds were due.

Companies that trade at large discounts to NAV often use excuses that their stakes are strategic (I'm not quite sure what that means, but I think it means, 'Don't ask more questions about this') and make the argument that they can add more value to their stakes than individual shareholders can. That a company trades at a big discount to the value of its holdings suggests otherwise, but importantly the discount also sets the bar that any new potential or current investment has to clear before making sense for the shareholders: if you can buy your own shares 40 per cent cheap, you had better have a really good reason for buying something else. If you bought your own shares, you would certainly have bought something that was 40 per cent cheap, and in the process of doing so would have made it cheaper yet (in the example above, the remaining shares would trade at a larger discount).

12

A day in the life

The following represents my experience of a typical day as a hedge-fund manager.

6.15am   Wake up. I am using my mobile as alarm clock and since it is in the charger 10 feet away, the snooze button is out of reach. Swiped alarm clock off the night table a while back and broke it. Those who say you get used to the early mornings are filthy liars.

6.35   Leave home for a brisk walk from Notting Hill to Mayfair through the park. Often hope for rain so that in good conscience I can take an eight-minute £7 taxi ride to South Molton Street coffee shop for my espresso fix instead of walking, before heading to office.

7.10   Arrive at Holte Capital. Turn on my three computer screens and the world of finance springs into life. All the news sources are set up on my screens so I know within seconds what's happening in the world and in the markets. Our stocks have tickers entered so flashes will appear if there is any news on them. Within a few minutes I will have an idea of what is going on including checking subject lines of emails from brokers. Nothing. So could have stayed in bed longer. Good joke from friend with link to YouTube which I check out when nobody sees me doing it.

7.50   Contact our trader to send orders that we want to work today in case they reach the prices we are looking for. Settle down to read a large industry report on oilrigs that I have been looking forward to.

7.52   Another phone call from broker to go over daily news, which I
          know already. I don't need this, and tell him so.

8.00   Opening auctions for most European markets.

8.07   Trader tells me one of our stocks is acting funny. Up a lot on
          heavy volume. Both she and I start calling around to hear what is
          going on.

8.12   Excellent. Up $1.2 million. Nice – at that rate I will be Bill Gates
          by the afternoon even if the profit is less than 0.5 per cent of our
          current AUM.

8.27   Company that was up a lot denies local radio rumours that they will
          be taken over; they want to stay independent. Stock in freefall and I
          am pissed off that I missed an opportunity to sell some shares.

8.32   Down $500K on the day now. Nothing good lasts forever – or in
          this case, more than 20 minutes. I try to go back to reading rig
          report in slight annoyed state, but phone keeps ringing with people
          trying to tell us that rumours of takeover are not true. Make a call
          to my contact at the company to hear if their tone has changed
          over being open for a takeover, but end up leaving a voicemail. He
          always told me that some of the other senior people seemed keen
          to cash out and I want to know if that has changed.

9.00   Potential recruit John is here on time. We are trying to hire an
          analyst and this one has a decent résumé. I like him, especially
          his story about climbing Mount McKinley in Alaska, something
          I always wanted to do. Ask why he left his previous hedge fund
          and John tells me that although his performance was excellent,
          he quit because he and the portfolio manager wanted to focus on
          different things. Why does nobody ever admit to losing money or
          getting fired? I don't catch him out on the bullshit story because
          he has some interesting trades he is talking about. Besides, I
          know John's former boss and can get the real story if we move
          down the road with him. Doriana knocks on the glass walls of
          the conference room to gesture that I should take a call. I bid
          John goodbye and call in Alberto. Alberto is our pit bull who
          loves digging into the analytical skills of recruits. I get to play the
          nice guy and have Alberto find out if they can add and subtract or
          know how to do a cash flow analysis.

10.20   Was I in there for over an hour? Must get more focused. I start going through the 15 emails that made it through the filter since I went into meeting and print out three reports to read later. Our trader Sarah asks if I want to change the limit on one of our trades since it is so close but we are getting nothing done. I tell her to use her best judgement. Also return call to our lawyer. He wanted to tell me about the latest tax planning scheme. I hear too many of those and thankfully have Brian to sort through them.

11.00   We are just about flat for the day so every couple of seconds P&L is blinking with a small black number to say we are up, then with red numbers to say we are losing money. Black – red – red – black – black. It can become hypnotic. I turn off the automatic update function on my computer and now it will only recalculate the P&L when I hit F9. I still hit F9 much too often. Only on page 7 of the rig report which is 42 pages long, but now I am making progress.

11.30   Leave for noon lunch in the city with company management for Dutch IT provider. I am heading there with Andy, a friend who works at a large US fund in Mayfair. We chat about trades in the taxi and discuss the crazy housing bubble in London. Something is going to have to give and I would not want to own a mortgage bank when it does. Lunch is near the top floor of Tower 42, one of the tallest buildings in London. It has a beautiful view south across the River Thames and all the way to green hills where the world of finance does not dominate every second of the day. I recognise a couple of faces and we nod acknowledgement. The CEO basically reads from the presentation and some of the guests have a hard time staying awake, including me. I should have had them come to our offices, but I sometimes like going to the group lunches so I can hear the questions from other managers and see how management presents.

1.30pm   Back in the office. P&L now up $500K which is better, but does not rock my world.

1.35   Call Puk to tell her that I will not be home for dinner. She told me I had promised to have dinner with her and her mum who is visiting town. I say sorry and promise to make it up. 'You always say that,' she says.

2.10   Resumed my rig report, but Oliver wants to talk about a new banking trade. If you eliminate the listed US and Polish units from Bank of Ireland, the remaining Irish domestic businesses trade much higher than their local competitors despite a very similar business profile. We could short Bank of Ireland, go long the two subsidiaries and the cheaper Irish competitors to lock in the spread. Sounds interesting, but Oliver has been on a bad run of losing trades and I need to look at this more closely before committing.

'But it is at such good levels now,' he says, still standing by my desk. I stall him again, then wonder whether I should go through Oliver's analysis before finishing my rig report. I don't want him to think I'm ignoring him.

2.46   I have a headache and try to kill it with my fifth coffee of the day. I can't focus on my report and keep getting my semi-submersible oilrigs confused so I take a ten-minute Internet 'break' and check out CNN and an interesting article in *NY Times* magazine. Bloomberg is great for that. Even if you are reading a Bloomberg article on football, the screen setup looks exactly the same as if you were reading work stuff and nobody can tell you are not working.

3.15   Analyst for one of our bigger investors calls for a quick update. Just wants to know what made and lost money last month so he can put it in his internal report. I worry slightly when he tells me that a lot of other funds did similarly to us last month. 'We don't want to correlate,' I think. He tells us again that they would be keen for us to take more risk.

4.05   Zach, another of our analysts, tells me he is '200 per cent certain' that a German company will dividend out their large cash holding and that the resulting entity will be bought by Deutsche Telecom and that we should act now. A couple of days ago he was only 110 per cent sure of something that did not happen, so 200 per cent is clearly better. I once told him that I considered something 90–95 per cent likely and he clearly understood that to mean a 50/50 chance. I enjoy making fun of each other over the way we express things, but get annoyed when it leads to misunderstandings in real probability calculations.

4.25   Closing auctions start. Quiet day, but we ended with a small $250K profit. Not quite a rounding error but close. There won't be many trades for Doriana to book into the system, which is just as well as we have a cake surprise ready for her birthday. I doubt it will be a real surprise as she is normally the one to get the cake when it is somebody else's birthday. Means I will have to skip my closing-bell Starbucks run.

4.47   Sit down with one of the guys to discuss insurance trade. We have kept track of the portfolio of a UK insurance company and notice that the value of their investment portfolio has fallen far more than the value of the company. We study in detail the duration of their bond portfolio as we think there is a mismatch with the company's longer-term insurance liabilities. We also note that they are involved with all sorts of default swaps that they have no business being involved in – typically a bad sign. We agree that there is a trade here at some point.

5.55   Brian asks me to sit in on a call with Morgan. Someone there says he has a philosophical issue with reducing a certain fee even if it is easy in practical terms. I tell him that I doubt Credit Suisse has philosophical or other issues with it and he reluctantly concedes the point. Probably a good thing we now have two competing prime brokers, even if it means our relationship will be less close.

6.30   Leaving the office to have drinks with a friend before dinner with a broker. I managed to read 32 pages of my rig report, which is better than some days. My friend is thinking about starting a hedge fund and tells me how he plans to raise $50 million through friends and family and then build a track record before going to $400 million and up from there. I am irritated by the implication that, 'If you could do it then surely anyone can.' If I had a dollar for every time someone has told me that exact plan . . .

7.45   I go back to the office to pick up the other guys and we go to dinner at a nice French restaurant with a Swiss broker who turns up 10 minutes after us. Why do these dinners always have to start at 8pm when most of us finish our work day at 6.30 or 7pm and are keen to get home on the early side? It's almost as if the broker does not think we can have a good time unless we leave the restaurant around 11pm having drunk too much. Really nice guy though – knows how to keep conversation flowing easily. Brought along a couple of younger guys who are clearly being trained in client entertainment. Main guy talks about a couple of trades, but those we are interested in we already know much better than the 30-second spin he gives us, and the rest are not really what we are looking for. Worth a try though.

11.30 Home in bed. Fall asleep before I hit the pillow.

The above account represents a hypothetical composite day, drawn from real experiences. While it gives, I believe, a realistic flavour of the daily Holte Capital routine, it fails to convey that one of the great things about running a hedge fund was enjoying the diversity of challenges that each day brought. And it only hints at the higher personal costs. When my wife Puk gave birth to our twin girls, Anna and Sofia, in December 2004, I was back at my desk within 48 hours and for the first three years of their lives I rarely saw them between the time we tucked them in on Sunday night and the moment we woke them the following Saturday morning. I left the house before they got up, and returned in the evening after they had gone to bed. Some Saturday mornings in the early days, my daughters would give me the puzzled look they would normally reserve for strangers, whereas friends of mine would proudly describe how close they were to their kids.

Running a hedge fund was obviously a 24/7 proposition, but I was also guilty of being unable to disconnect. When we took our rare holidays I would constantly be on the computer to deal with some real or perceived crisis at the office. I would frequently find excuses to call in to hear what the daily P&L looked like. Eventually I decided that the best way to save me from myself was to go west for family holidays. In the Caribbean, the London trading day would be half done by the time we got out of bed in the morning and despite my best efforts to ruin my own holiday there were only so many hours left in the day to do so before the markets closed for the day. By contrast, if we were in Egypt or Dubai, Puk would comment on how I seemed absent-minded as we sat down to dinner – while I was thinking about the closing market auctions that would be going on right then.

> Running a hedge fund was obviously a 24/7 proposition, but I was also guilty of being unable to disconnect.

Although the stress of running a hedge fund was unusually high during the week, the working hours were no longer than those of my peers from business school and I would rarely work weekends. Comparing this with my investment banker or consulting friends, the whole thing was really a bit of a breeze . . . right!

Despite the predictable sacrifices, I loved the freedom my job offered, and considered myself incredibly lucky. I did what I found interesting instead of being a cog in a corporate wheel where my time would effectively be allocated by others. I remember often laughing to myself at the stark contrast between my time at Holte Capital and my early days as an analyst in the dungeons of Lazard Frères when my typical day would go something like this:

8.30am   Turn up in your sharpest suit ready to be one of this generation's masters of the universe. You hope nobody notices you are wearing the suit for the fifth day running.

If busy or caught not looking busy:

9am–11pm or later   Get screamed at by sadist superiors often out for revenge for the torture they endured while they were in your lowly position a couple of years ago. Make small formatting adjustments in the endless spreadsheets you produce at their pleasure. If I never see another 50-page Excel model with thousands of numbers in varying colours and shades again it will be too soon. Pressure slows when your immediate boss checks out around 10pm, his boss having checked out at 9.30pm, leaving you to complete 'something we need for tomorrow'.

One night around midnight after about eight months at Lazard I was frantically trying to complete a spreadsheet. I knew the partner on the deal was waiting impatiently in his office. Twice already my phone had rung with the phone display screaming: 'BRAD EVANS'. What it should really have said was 'BRAD EVANS. ANGRY PARTNER. EATS BABIES FOR FUN'. He was not happy being kept in the office by a young analyst when he should have had an associate and vice-president buffering his exposure to my youth and inexperience. I finished the last part of the analysis, did a quick double-check and ran downstairs to present my work with the printout still warm in my hand.

Brad took the analysis from me without uttering a word. He seemed content as he went over the numbers. Suddenly his demeanour changed to a dour expression and he pulled out his calculator. 'Oh no,' I thought, knowing what would come next. He circled a number with a fat blue pen and in pre-rage mode said between gritted teeth: 'This number is wrong. You'll need to do it again.'

'Sorry,' I said. 'There must be a bad link in my spreadsheet.'

'SORRY!?' he yelled contemptuously, before screaming: 'DON'T BE SORRY. BE RIGHT FOR FUCK'S SAKE. IF THAT NUMBER IS WRONG HOW DO I KNOW THAT ANY NUMBERS ARE RIGHT? THIS IS USELESS SHIT, LARS. BAD, BAD, BAD.'

At this point I was already leaving his office half-expecting him to hurl something at me. Ten feet from his office was where the night-shift word processing staff was sitting. Most of them were aspiring actors or musicians who took the job to pay the bills. A couple of them had been working on the supporting slides for our presentation. They all looked at me as I approached them after my verbal beating and the first guy I approached said: 'Dude. Nothing can be worth that. He talked to you like you were a dog.'

Note to self: Despite putting needles in voodoo dolls of my immediate bosses at the time, I can't believe that some of those slave masters from the dark side are friends today . . .

If not busy

Rule number 1: Look busy

9am–6pm	Same shit. We did not yet have Internet access in 1994 so we could not surf the net. Bummer. One guy read *War and Peace* inside a research report.
6pm–7:30pm	Go to the gym. Leave your jacket on the chair so it looks like you have just stepped away for a moment and make sure your screensaver is deactivated. These were the pre-mobile phone days so once you escaped the building you were safe.
7.30pm	Order food. Make sure you order with people who will be too busy to eat so you can use their dinner allowance and get yourself some nice sushi and the miniscule pyrrhic victory that come with eating well alone in a dull conference room.

9pm   Order car. Take the fire escape stairs down a couple of
               floors so nobody sees you leaving the office early and thus
               avoid the 5pm call from the staffing person on Friday tell-
               ing you that you have been put on a new project.

PART THREE

On the front line

13

Getting fully examined

A $100-million near miss

By its third year of operation in 2005 Holte Capital was managing close to $300 million and was decidedly the real thing. Long gone were the reservations about my being too young to run a portfolio. Those who had tracked us for a while were getting comfortable with the consistency of our approach and analysis. We were delivering returns that were uncorrelated to the markets and although the return profile was boring we could justifiably claim that we were slowly augmenting our risk profile, making it more interesting for our investors.

One of the largest US banks had been talking for a while about opening a managed account and they clearly seemed keen. A managed account is a separate entity from the main fund that tries to replicate the securities in the main fund, yet remains owned by the investor. We as the managers would receive normal fees and have complete control over the account, but to make up for the slightly larger administrative and trading hassles involved in having such an account we indicated that it would have to be a substantial investment in the context of our then approximately $300 million AUM. They came back to us a couple of days after I had had an hour-long conference call with Jake Nelson, head of investment banking and a board member, and said they would like to make a $100-million investment. We were thrilled. The more junior guys responsible for the investment showed the normal unease before my call with Jake. If I made a terrible impression they would look bad internally for having suggested me as an investment.

They prepped me with the kinds of questions Jake normally liked to ask and prepared me for his style. Clearly at that stage they were more concerned that I looked good to Jake than if Holte Capital provided a good investment opportunity. As I sometimes found to be the case when speaking to very senior people among potential investor firms, I remember being somewhat underwhelmed by the call. The questions and dialogue was friendly enough, but in terms of understanding Holte and our investment style, other people had shown far greater insight. I put it down to the guy being busy and he did not want to undermine his team by rejecting a Holte investment anyway.

After a couple of years of large growth we had wanted to make a step change into the billion-dollar fund range and this was the kind of investor who would help make that happen. Because of the nature of a managed account (legally speaking, it is like another fund) there were lots of lawyers involved and at around $900 an hour they were only too eager to help. The first sign of trouble came when Dennis Lyle, our main contact at the bank, took four hours to return a call from me asking when the money was due to hit the account. With days to go before making a $100-million investment, I had expected him to call me back promptly, unless his house was on fire. Unfortunately, in a sense, it was.

'Hi Lars. It's Dennis.' He sounded hesitant, as if there was someone standing next to him.

'Hi Dennis. Everything OK?'

'Well, yes. All good . . . actually perhaps not. Don't really know. There are all these people on our floor today. I recognised a couple of them from our website. Senior management. Who knows – perhaps we are getting bought and all my options will be worth a fortune,' Dennis said, clearly not knowing what to believe. I asked him about the portfolio and we discussed the best way to scale into some of the securities to get best execution for the account. We had moved on to discuss currency hedging when he interrupted me mid-sentence. 'Hang on a minute. There's someone here to see me.' A long pause, then: 'I gotta call you back,' and he hung up. When I called back 45 minutes later, the phone went straight to voicemail. I went home without having heard back from him.

The following morning there was an email from Dennis in my inbox. It said:

'Incredible news. The guy who came to my office was part of the human resources group. They fired the whole group all the way up to Jake. Can't believe it. Sounds like they are unwinding the group and outsourcing hedge-fund investing. Not sure what this means for our Holte investment. Hope we can stay in touch!'

I wrote him back the obligatory 'Of course we are going to stay in touch' email and offered to ask around to see if there was anyone looking to hire.

Later in the day I received an email from the bank's general counsel's office saying that the bank had decided to suspend all investment activities for their hedge-fund investing group and that the investment in Holte Capital would be put on hold as a result. It pointed to language in our contract with them which allowed the bank to reverse the investment decision until the monies had been wired, but offered to pay us any expenses we had incurred in legal and administrative preparation for the investment – an offer we declined as the expenses (even at $900 an hour) were minimal in the context of maintaining good relations with a bank that had almost invested $100 million with Holte.

As ever, Brian had a healthy perspective. 'We are ready for the big time and although this was a bad blow, there was nothing we could do about it. If we keep performing, there will be lots of other large investors knocking on the door. The fact that we came that close to $100 million means we must be doing something right.'

At the time four of the world's ten largest investors in hedge funds had invested with Holte Capital. They had each invested a relatively small amount in their terms. Even an average investment of $50 million is not that big if you are managing more than $10 billion, which all of them were. But the positive we could take from these four investors was that they had all overcome the hurdle of deciding to invest with Holte and they would each be able to increase their investment to hundreds of millions of dollars if they wished. That in turn meant that we could concentrate on keeping our existing investors happy rather than spending time and effort trying to attract new investors. This was a novel concept for me, after years of selling my soul in a standard pitch to anyone who cared to listen – and many who didn't.

Fifty million dollars is a lot of money. There is something almost intimidating about the fact that someone decided to

Fifty million dollars is a lot of money.

give that money to you rather than anyone else in the world. They could have found the next Google or Facebook and multiplied their money a hundred times or invested with any of the emerging markets funds that were up 50 per cent last year. But they chose Holte Capital instead. Once Holte Capital had grown to the size where the investments were generally larger than $10 million, people began to scrutinise my background in remarkable detail. Long gone were the days when potential investors would call my former bosses and trust them when they said I was a nice guy. Increasingly, larger potential investors did their own checks. I would occasionally get the odd email from someone I knew years ago to say that so and so had been in touch to ask what I was like in college, if I used to have a drug problem, or if I had really been a scratch golfer. Clearly those who invested overcame whatever misdeeds they found in my past, but I have always been curious to hear about those who did the checks and subsequently declined to invest. What did they find? I tell myself they must have found something dodgy in Brian's past, not mine.

These were among the discoveries made about me:

1 Outstanding parking tickets from place I used to live.
   (I had no idea – honest.)

2 Puk had not paid her T-Mobile phone bill when she left Denmark and moved to New York to live with me.
   (So I guess I married into debt…)

3 I had not renewed my Massachusetts driving licence and had not taken a new one in another US state.
   (I moved to the UK before my licence expired.)

4 I appeared in a *Cosmopolitan* magazine article about what eligible New York bachelors find attractive in a woman.
   (Not my proudest moment, and of course I was misquoted.)

5 I was caught buying alcohol in the US under the age of 21.
   (No comment – except that our European attitudes are rather more liberal.)

6 I was related to the famous Danish painter.
   (Not true. The painter is spelled Kroyer and we are Kroijer. Could have been true, though, because we were apparently spelled like the painter until a priest put two dots over the 'y' on a marriage certificate ages ago.)

7 I was president of a gay club at Harvard.

(Odd one. Not true – I am straight – but I was offended that they consid-ered it their business. I was president of a Harvard final club which is an all-male fraternity. This one turned out to be a joke from a friend in a rival final club.)

8 I almost moved to Mongolia.

(I applied for a summer job with the Ministry of Privatisation in Mongolia.)

9 I lied about graduating with honours from Harvard Business School.

(Slightly embarrassing. I got what was called second-year honours – based on grades – and I thought that was the same as graduating with honours. I'm still not sure if it is and didn't particularly care about grades at HBS anyway, but to this guy graduating with honours was apparently some-thing different.)

10 I changed my name.

(True. I used to be Lars Kroijer-Jensen, but when I was quite young my mother dropped the name 'Jensen' for all of us as it is the most common sur-name in Denmark and I was constantly being called Lars Jensen. Lars was also the most used first name at the time. I was not particularly fussed but I guess in the pre-Google days it was nice to have a more distinctive surname.)

The whole game of background checking is going to change tremendously with the increasing strength of data mining or search engines and social websites like Facebook. They will make it harder to hide unsavoury parts of your past. This is the main reason I keep telling people to avoid suing former counterparties, partners or employees. Even if you win the law-suit, you might end up explaining in detail for years to come why a Google search said you had been involved in a lawsuit. You might have to fight off the suspicion that you may be a litigious person. I compare it to trying to explain to an immigration officer at JFK airport why you were really inno-cent when you had your visa revoked on your last visit and that he should let you through so you can make your meeting in Manhattan in 30 min-utes. Oh, and pay your parking tickets.

Funds of funds

Investing in hedge funds is not an amateur's game. Even if you manage to avoid investing with the small minority of funds that engage in dubious practices, the sparse disclosure most funds offer to smaller private investors leaves you vulnerable to not knowing enough about the investment you have undertaken. If investing in hedge funds is not your full-time job or you don't have enough capital to invest in several funds at once, funds of funds may well be the answer. Along with the massive growth in the hedge-fund industry over the past decade, the number of funds of funds and the assets they manage have exploded.

Funds of funds are simply funds that invest in other (hedge) funds. The size and strategy of each fund of funds varies greatly, although there tends to be a concentration of larger funds of funds, probably because they enjoy the advantage of scale. It is an expensive business researching hedge funds and performing the necessary due diligence on each one – which must put quite a strain on the resources of the smaller funds of funds.

At Holte Capital most of our investors were very large funds of funds, and I found their quality varied enormously, from those that had no business looking after other people's money to those that were at the top of their game. The best had a clear command of a number of strategies and a real understanding of the risk involved in each individual strategy as well as how those risks related to each other. A quality fund of funds would understand if a hedge fund had made its returns simply by owning a raising market in a geared way. This would indicate if the hedge fund had added value or was just along for the ride in a strong market. There would be real analysis of the hedge fund's trades and an attempt to find risks the managers had not thought of themselves. The fund of funds would then be able to create a portfolio of top-performing funds that fitted together well from a risk perspective so that the overall portfolio would be well diversified and appropriate to the chosen risk profile.

I used to think that working for a fund of funds would be a fantastic job as you get paid to talk to really clever people who are highly engaged in their work and keen to sell their product to you. What is there not to like? Some friends who work for funds of funds do seem to enjoy the process of digging out interesting managers and new hedge-fund strategies, but they also bemoan the monotony of the presentations that all look and sound the same. One friend described going to a conference tasked with looking at nine different hedge-fund managers in one day.

▶

'You sit there for just under an hour and actually speak very little. The managers all have charts and graphs with bubbles and arrows going everywhere and long lists of their special edge in the market, all called something from a business-school textbook like "our alpha machine" or "our sustainable competitive advantage". You usually find many of the hedge-fund managers self-absorbed and arrogant, clearly having been told a few too many times how smart and special they are by all the brokers and counterparties. Those that have been on a good run and don't really need more investments treat you with thinly veiled contempt for not having invested when they needed it. They love saying things like, "Perhaps we can find room for you in the future". By the ninth meeting, you are exhausted and can't remember who said what. I took to writing on the presentations what the manager looked like or what he wore, but they always seemed to say, "Around 40, blue shirt & khakis, white guy, glasses". I am glad it was not the text for a dating site. But then once in a while you come across something unique that you don't think the world and the million other funds of funds have discovered and you immediately get the focused attention of a super-smart guy who might have found a better mousetrap.'

The problem with funds of funds is obviously the extra layer of fees. Although some larger investors can get discounts, the funds of funds typically charge 1 per cent in annual management fee and a 10 per cent incentive fee on top of certain expenses. You add this to the high hedge-fund fees and quickly realise that the net returns to the funds of funds investor are only realised after a lot of khaki-clad white guys have taken their bite. But if you want to invest money with hedge funds and either do not have a unique angle on a specific fund or cannot afford the staff to investigate the alternatives full time, top-quality funds of funds are probably well worth the fees.

14

Blood in the streets

The London bombing

From my perspective as a hedge-fund trader the 7 July 2005 bombings on London were quite different from the 11 September attacks in the USA four years earlier. The instant the second plane hit the World Trade Center in New York, the world knew that there had been a substantial terrorist attack and that the implications would be severe and long-lasting. The futures on the US stock indices that were trading even before the general market had opened immediately started to plummet. The London bombings were different. The first indication I received that something was amiss was an email message from a broker that there were signal problems and some tumult at Liverpool Street tube station. 'What else is new?' was my reaction as I went back to my day thinking, 'I hope this does not make Anne late for her appointment at Bloomberg.' My younger sister Anne had been spending her summer as an intern at Holte Capital and had planned an 8.30am appointment at Bloomberg near Liverpool Street station to have a tutorial on the platform.

Within a minute there was another email from a broker who was clearly keen to get the news out first: 'Smoke coming from Liverpool St'. Already, the unfolding events reminded me of the first message I had received four years earlier that something was wrong in New York when a broker looking out of his midtown Manhattan office simply wrote 'WTC on fire'. I tried calling my sister's mobile, but there was no signal. I guessed she must still be on the Underground and thought nothing more of it.

Soon a couple of news sources started to pick up a story of extensive delays on the London Underground with bottlenecks in several locations. 'How annoying for her' I thought as I noticed that the stock index had gone down a little. Then a newsflash read 'EXPLOSION ON LONDON BUS'. My heart sank and I remember lifting my hands to my chest like a boxer ready to defend myself, thinking, 'Shit, this is terrorism and multiple hits'. Since there was no news of casualties other than talk of some injured people at Liverpool Street, the situation did not have the terrifying visual impact that the New York attacks did.

One news source confirmed that there was at least one fatality at Liverpool Street and a confirmed explosion near Edgware Road. Now about 45 minutes had passed and I had continuously tried to reach my sister, but the mobile networks were down due to the large amount of traffic. I thought of heading to Liverpool Street by foot, but soon discounted that idea – the whole area was bound to be sealed off and the chances of finding my sister in the hordes of confused people were negligible. I was glancing at the portfolio sporadically and happy we were flat in what was now a significantly falling market – our hedges were working. Then the picture of the bus bombing hit the news websites. The roof of the double-decker bus had been blown off, leaving the upper deck exposed to the open air like one of the sightseeing buses you see around London. The reaction in the office was swift and unanimous. This is far worse than the injury and fatality reports currently suggested in the press. There were still no official death reports from the bus attack, yet it was clear to me that an explosion powerful enough to blow off the roof in the busy rush-hour traffic would have taken many lives. If there were no reports, yet obvious casualties on the bus, what did this suggest about the other explosions?

I was beginning to panic. Why did her phone not work? I had got through to Puk's mobile to tell her to turn on the TV and stay indoors with the kids, but my sister was still not picking up hers. It had now been an hour since the first explosion and the number of confirmed dead was rising all the time. 'Please let her not be hurt,' I prayed, while frantically trying to work out how I could find out more about her fate. There was no point in calling the hospitals or going there – I would have no idea where to start. Walking the streets looking for her would be equally pointless – she would know to return to the office or get in touch if she could. I had got through to the contact person at Bloomberg she was supposed to meet who confirmed that she had not turned up for their appointment.

Obviously, I feared the worst as the death toll continued to rise. There were now about 20 people confirmed dead, but the journalists expected that to increase. I decided that minute that if something had happened to my sister I would leave London and return home to Denmark to live with my family. 'It ends here,' I thought. My colleagues were trying to comfort me, saying that there were literally millions of people in and around the city so the chances were that my sister was just fine. I was about to call my parents in Denmark to say that there had been a terrorist attack and that I could not get hold of Anne when the elevator made the familiar 'ding' and she walked out on the floor as if it was any other morning. I didn't say anything as the others gathered around her but wiped my sweaty fore-head and smiled with relief. Anne had been stuck in the train after the one that had been attacked on Liverpool Street and had walked out through the pitch-black tunnels to the street above. Someone from the Underground had mentioned something about a faulty train ahead and she had assumed nothing more serious. After trying a couple of times to get through to the person at Bloomberg she was supposed to meet she had decided to walk all the way back through central London to our offices in Mayfair. Although she clearly knew that something unusual was happening, she was shocked to hear that there had been a multiple bomb attack on London.

We spent the rest of the day in disbelief at what had happened, aware that another strike could happen any minute. We did very little trading, partly because our focus was elsewhere, but also because our trades were more or less hedged and provided no great trading opportunity. After the markets closed for business we decided to email our investors to say that while our thoughts were with those directly affected by today's bombing, our portfolio had not been affected and we were flat for the day.

In the weeks and months after the London bombing the city was in a constant state of fear of another attack. Our office was near the popu-lar shopping street Bond Street and the US embassy in Grosvenor Square, both likely targets for another attack. We debated whether we had an obli-gation to our investors to try to benefit from this. If there was another attack on London it would probably lead to sudden large losses on the stock exchange. If, through our location near the centre of such an attack, we knew about it even seconds before the wider market, we could bene-fit from that knowledge by selling the broader market or individual stocks before they plummeted. Was this amoral? If indeed there was a terrorist attack so close to us that we could hear it, would we not be morally obliged to run down and see if there was anything we could do to help the victims instead of remaining in our comfortable chairs and profiting from it?

I continued my mental exercise. In our single-minded scramble to accumulate fees or build the perfect portfolio, had we hedge-fund managers become oblivious to the rest of humanity? Within an hour of the second plane hitting the World Trade Center and the devastation clear to all, I remember two guys giving each other an enthusiastic high-five since they had randomly bought credit default protection against an airline shortly before the attack (insurance against the airline's defaulting on its debt), the value of which had surged as it was clear that the outlook for airlines had materially worsened as a result of the attack. One of those was the most unquestionably patriotic American you could find, yet his momentary enthusiasm over a great trade ranked higher than his concern for fellow citizens. On the other hand, I was also troubled by my own instinctive reaction to contemplate moving to Denmark if something bad happened – was this a sign of healthy perspective, or a lack of serious commitment to running my business in London? I concluded the former, but questions still lingered.

Somewhat sheepishly, we decided to create a 'disaster stock list'. This was a list of 20 European shares (some traded in the USA in case an attack happened after the European markets closed) that would be particularly hard hit by a London terrorist attack. These included British Airways, the insurance companies, banks, and hotel businesses. We set up the system so that we could sell a certain amount of each stock within seconds of deciding to do so, and only if the stock had not dropped more than a couple of per cent already, in case we were too late. We kept this list ready on our direct market-access platform and were ready to hit the button at a moment's notice. I remember feeling particularly bad about doing this, but reasoned that it was part of being a profit-hungry hedge fund in a highly competitive marketplace; if we did not sell the shares, somebody else would. Mayer Rothschild once famously said, 'Buy when there is blood in the streets', suggesting that investors should buy at the time of peak panic and despair. Instead, we would be *selling* when there was blood in the streets, just before the wider market knew that it was there.

Thankfully, our 'merchant of death' trade was never put into place.

15

Edge

The elusive 'edge'

Once potential investors have satisfied themselves that you are not a crook, the single question they most often ask is, 'What is your edge?' They want to know how you think you can beat the competition. And we all have an answer. You have to. You can't justify charging investors to manage their money if you cannot explain why investing with you is any better than a monkey throwing darts. Answers you hear often from managers are things like 'forensic accounting', 'primary research', 'a proven proprietary trading system', 'a better process' and so on. It is no wonder that investors are sometimes unable to decipher the jargon and fall back on investing with companies that have the best performance history. 'Nobody ever got fired for buying IBM,' as they used to say.

> Once potential investors have satisfied themselves that you are not a crook, the single question they most often ask is, 'What is your edge?'

Many investors asked about our competition. We would try to deflect the questions by discussing our approach instead and saying that although many others analysed similar situations, our rigorous use of hedging made us unique. Some of our investors tried to put us into their various investment buckets of 'special situations', 'long/short', 'distressed funds', etc. 'We're more of a square peg in a round hole,' we would tell them, even though we tended to make money in months where others did well and lose when other funds lost money.

The truth is that our competition was everyone and no one. If we could provide the 8–12 per cent annual returns completely independent of the markets or other funds, we would not have to worry about competition. If we really were uncorrelated to anything and had positive returns, there would always be room for Holte in any investor's portfolio. For a while we were convinced that this was true, but when the dust eventually settled, it wasn't.

At Holte, we felt our combination of fundamental value analysis and event assessment gave us a unique angle from which we could generate superior returns. We would use our hedging strategy to create exactly the investment we believed was mispriced and our trades often looked very convoluted as a result (like being long one stock and short four others against it in different currencies). Our high success rate suggested that something was working somewhere. However, like everyone else, we were always looking for better ways of doing things. About three years into the life of the fund, this quest led us down the path of pair trading of local companies in two truly global industries.

> At Holte, we felt our combination of fundamental value analysis and event assessment gave us a unique angle from which we could generate superior returns.

A Holte mousetrap

It was evolution of our existing strategy that led to our becoming involved in the shipping and oilrig industries. We were looking at the Danish product tanker company Torm (transporting refined oil) which owned a stake in dry bulk company D/S Norden (transporting things like iron ore, grains, etc.). We were trying to deduct the Norden stake from Torm and compare the remaining product tanker company with its peers.

Soon a picture emerged. Since oil tankers have a finite life of around 25 years and are used for a certain number of days a year, you can get a good idea of the value of a tanker if you know the all-important day rate that the tanker company charges for renting out the vessel. And there's the rub. Over the last five years the day rate of the largest standard oil tanker (the VLCC – very large crude carrier) has varied from roughly

$12,000 per day to as much as $250,000. With a fairly fixed cost structure, the extra money goes straight to the bottom line. This explains the
massive share-price volatility of some of the large shipping companies. If
you lose money one year and have a profit margin like Microsoft's the
next, your share price is bound to be volatile. But what we cared about
more than absolute returns were the relative performances of the various
industry players.

We looked at about 14 oil-tanker companies with a focused asset base
and noticed a trend: although the rates to rent the tankers fluctuated
wildly, the relative rates of the various vessel types remained more or less
constant over time. This made sense as the amount of oil a ship could
transport was fixed. So with basic assumptions about utilisation, labour,
upkeep, costs, etc. we could create a standard model that allowed us to
compare oil tanker companies. We built a massive Excel model where
we had whole fleets for each of the companies, down to the specifics of
each ship, and used it to measure the value of a fleet, given various input
assumptions on rates at which they would be charged out.

What we found was very interesting. As you would expect, the
market value of the assets (fleets) of these companies varied quite a bit.
Particularly interesting was how the stocks moved relative to each other
in a highly volatile market once you adjusted for their respective gearing
to changes in the day rate. While the short-term fluctuations appeared
random at times, over the medium term there seemed to be a large
degree of mean-reversion. This made sense. Once we had adjusted for a
few other factors, we were able to compare like with like and the things

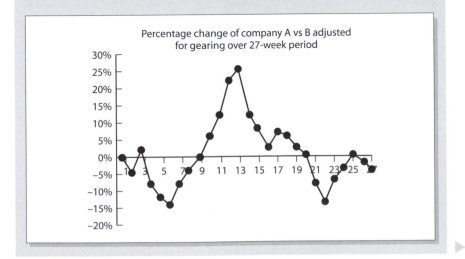

that drove one company up were likely to have a similar impact on related companies, even if short-term market fluctuations suggested otherwise.

So we created a portfolio of pairs of shipping companies that seemed to be out of line both from a valuation basis and historical trading range. Each pair tried to be neutral to changes in shipping rates, currencies or markets. As an example, we would be long $10 of one stock and short $15 of another. Since the $10 we were long was geared higher than the $15 stock we were short, the trade was still market-neutral. And, since it does not get much more international than oil shipping, we relished cross-border trades. A company listed in New York may be very similar to a Greek company listed in Oslo, but the two stock markets may be very different in the short term. And that was when Holte Capital pounced.

Once the trades in the shipping sector seemed to be working fairly consistently, we moved on to oilrigs. Like oil tankers, oilrigs are finite assets that operate in an international market and there are a small number of stock exchange-listed companies (they are mainly based in either Houston or Oslo). As with shipping, we created a massive financial model where we had all the data on individual rigs. We would have their age and type, along with the contracts. And then we would start to do the same relative pair trades that we had in shipping.

We thought these trades were working and that we had built a mouse-trap. No one else was thinking in these exact terms, we thought. Both the shipping and oilrig work required a massive initial investment of time and effort as well as the ability to work across time zones and currencies. I was very happy with our work. We were in this business to create a unique return profile based on superior analysis, and that was exactly what we were doing. I had really enjoyed examining the fine details of the trades and caught myself looking up from my desk thinking, 'This is why I do this'.

Unfortunately, we never managed to launch a separate shipping/oilrig fund. Despite the main fund achieving a decent size and making good returns, we never felt we had the momentum to present a new fund as a *fait accompli* to potential investors. Instead, they might have seen the launch as something that would distract us from running the main fund and take their assets away from it as a result. In retrospect, this fear was probably unfounded and we should just have gone ahead and launched a separate fund with a couple of investors. Our failure to launch this or another couple of separate funds was another example of Holte taking too little risk.

▶

I completely understand hedge-fund managers who try to launch separate funds. When you are managing only one fund you are incredibly vulnerable with one product to sustain your business, and bad performance can easily put you out of business, altogether. Diversifying across multiple funds and ensuring that they don't correlate gives you far greater durability when times are tough. Of course, if you diversify across five funds that are all very market-dependent there is really no diversification at all, as they all do poorly in a bear market – a lesson painfully learned by some managers in 2008.

16

Made it?

You are like a real fund now

By 2006, Holte Capital's assets under management had been fairly constant for a couple of years. After we reached $100 million in the fall of 2003 we had quickly taken on more money and moved to about $300 million, but after that our growth stagnated. Without meaning to, we had created a return profile stable enough that few investors ran for the hills, but too boring for hundreds of people to beat down the door to invest. This plateau of assets fell short of reaching the multiple-billion-dollar mega-fund territory, but Holte was still a highly profitable medium-sized hedge fund.

Being profitable for longer did lead to some stability in managing the business. After bringing in several new colleagues in the first couple of years we outgrew our office in Berkeley Square and moved to a large, professionally decorated office with high ceilings on Brook Street near the corner of Bond Street. The new space had a kitchen, glass conference room and office, and really looked the part. As a testament to Brian's organisation, I only saw the place once while it was being redecorated before the move. On Friday evening, we shut down our computers at the old office and turned up at the new address on Monday morning to find everything working beautifully.

In time, I also came to feel more like a proper boss. The early days of Holte Capital had been dominated by chaos and 'what on earth do we do now?' moments. After several years of running the fund, I had experienced most situations a couple of times before and had an instinctive idea of how to deal with them. Apart from captaining my school football team,

I had had no real experience of leadership until I was forced into the role at Holte. Decisions about everything from large-scale investments to small stuff had to be made in real time and my style probably ended up being somewhere between a friendly democratic mediator and autocratic dictator. But dithering with decisions was pointless. The issues were not going to go away. Some questions were incredibly important to the ongoing success of Holte Capital and others were more mundane, for example:

Are you OK to put $25 million in this trade now?

Should we offer a job to A or B?

Do we settle this trade at Morgan or Credit Suisse?

Should we get a coffee machine for the office? (Are you nuts? Drink instant!)

What shade of blue should our new logo be?

And endless other things. Gradually, I found that more and more of my time was spent negotiating these day-to-day issues rather than burying my head in investment reports. There were times when I left the office on a Friday evening after a long and stressful week and realised that I had done virtually no financial analysis that week, and that I missed it.

Besides making more money, our sustained higher size of assets under management had two other big benefits. We were starting to be recognised by others in the industry. The longer we were in business, the more people had heard of us. We were also in a better position to negotiate terms with our counterparties, as lots of their competitors now wanted our business. There were people who had ignored us in the early days but were now keen to get in touch – like Jay from Westbank, who called me one day to 'reconnect', despite having ignored three phone calls and four emails right after we launched.

'Listen,' said Jay. 'I wanted to swing by your new swanky office to go through what we are doing here. We have a great product suite both in execution and research that you can't live without. And I am sorry to see that we have not done any business with you since you left HBK.' I thought that might have had something to do with his not taking my calls, but kept it to myself.

'You guys are like a real fund now,' Jay continued. 'I mean, not that you weren't before . . . We were just so busy with good clients. Er, not that you would not have been good clients, of course!' I could sense his growing embarrassment at the other end of the phone, and after an awkward pause, I just laughed.

'Look, Jay,' I said. 'I know how it works. We were small and you have to hit your numbers. Don't worry about it. Let's just schedule the meeting and look ahead.'

It's much easier to be magnanimous when you are not worrying about how to make ends meet.

The greatest benefit of having more assets was having more people. With an average team size of seven, the higher fees meant we could pay the better performers a competitive package right away, not just give them a promise of future riches. Once we had a certain number of analysts working at Holte we had to come up with a formal structure for payouts. In 2005 we found that a fully discretionary bonus system had led to an expectation gap where I felt everyone got a fair bonus, but most people felt short-changed. It was a bad year for the firm. We had only been up around 5–6 per cent after fees, so the bonus pool was fairly small. The total bonus payments were approximately 70 per cent of the incentive fee with the remaining 30 per cent going to Brian and me, not only as the founders, but as CFO and Portfolio Manager too. While this split was probably fair, the numbers were not as large as some people had expected, and several were clearly unhappy. One pretended to have misheard me, and found himself on the end of a rare outburst.

'Look mate,' I said. 'You got paid the same as I did as an analyst in my previous job. The difference is that I had bought each of the partners a couple of Ferraris and you have just about bought me half a Volvo. Your attitude is, frankly, insulting.'

That particular analyst realised he had to back down or be sacked. What I hated most was the way people were constantly testing boundaries in the bonus conversations to see how much money they could get away with asking for – this seemed an ingrained part of the system that nobody was immune to. And yet I was often told by outsiders how we were known to be one of the more harmonious hedge funds where people genuinely got along. I kept reminding myself that I had been no different back when I was the bonus recipient rather than giver.

For all those who have been on the receiving end of bonus conversations and hated the uncertainty, I can assure them it is equally unpleasant to be the giver. It seems that few people are ever simply happy and thankful. Instead, they worry that their assent might suggest that they would be happy with a lower bonus next year.

The year after all this bonus aggravation, we instituted a system whereby the analysts received a certain fraction of what they earned for the firm and non-analysts were paid on the basis of the firm's assets and overall performance. To get an overall picture, I asked several friends who ran hedge funds what they did. Very roughly, it seemed that the typical split was that 50 per cent went to the capital providers, 25 per cent to the portfolio manager and 25 per cent to the analysts. The rest of the team was paid out of the management fee. The system I came up with generously allowed that the analysts would be paid 40–50 per cent of the incentive fee they generated on the trades they worked on, capped at two-thirds of the total bonus pool. The reason for the cap was that if someone lost a lot of money while someone else was highly profitable we did not want to end up with a net liability. As a small incentive to keep people at Holte, I made about a quarter of the payment a deferred bonus that would only be paid if the analyst was still at the firm two years later. I had not liked this system in my previous job, but now that I was in charge, I liked the idea of paying more to those who were loyal to the firm.

So in simple arithmetic, if you have four analysts (including the portfolio manager) managing $200 million and they each manage a similar amount, they should have $50 million in their portfolio of trades. If they generate a 10 per cent return on this, the incentive fee will be $1 million ($50 million × 10% return × 20% incentive fee). So their bonus would be $400,000–500,000 on top of a $150,000–200,000 base salary. Not too shabby, I would have thought. Now do the same sum if there is $500 million and only five analysts, or even $1 billion. The amounts quickly get astounding. An extension of the above argument is clearly how the really big money is made in the hedge-fund industry. Imagine a $10-billion fund with eight partners that after a good year has a 20 per cent return. With a standard hedge-fund fee structure the total annual fee income will be $600 million ($10 billion × 20% × 20% + $10 billion × 2%). All non-partner compensation and expenses can be covered with $50 million and keep them very happy, thus leaving a $550 million pie to share among the eight. So each of them will take home around $70 million that year and turn up on 1 January the following year and hope to do it again. And you wonder why the townhouses on the Upper East Side in New York or in Chelsea in London were so expensive before the bubble burst? This is Russian oligarch-level income and you were just one of eight partners in an anonymous investment firm with a funny name. Now imagine that the founding partner had half, and not one-eighth, of the $500-million pie, the fund was larger than $10 billion, or the return much greater than 20 per cent . . .

Nouveau riche

Running a fund with its quick changes from ecstasy to near-death, I often lost sight of the bigger picture. I would never look up from my desk and think, 'Cool, you've made it.' There was always another trade, the next monthly letter, or some disaster about to happen. But after several years my success was slowly starting to make an impact on my life.

> Running a fund with its quick changes from ecstasy to near-death, I often lost sight of the bigger picture.

After the twins were born, we moved to a large house in fashionable Notting Hill. It did not come cheap, but, for us, it was not a lot more to pay for a big step up in quality. It seemed as if all our new neighbours were rich foreigners, private-equity or hedge-fund investors, and perhaps the occasional banker. At these prices, you were unlikely to be a fireman or a teacher. The lack of people with 'normal' jobs created a somewhat unreal atmosphere. All the expensive restaurants in the area were filled with customers in perfect outfits. With my picture-perfect family and friends, I clearly blended right in. There was so much money around and it looked like it was always going to remain that way.

Getting our kids into the fancy private schools in the area made getting into Harvard seem like a formality. We heard a rumour that some women had timed their Caesarean sections to a certain time of month that gained them a favourable spot on the waiting list. Once when a friend from nursery was visiting our girls, she innocently asked them, 'Are you poor?' To her horror, she had discovered that the twins shared a bedroom, right after being told that we didn't have a summer house in the South of France for the weekends. No kidding. To add a bit of flash, our neighbour was the guy who ran and owned the Gumball rally. He was nice enough but with my old Honda in the driveway there was never going to be a true meeting of minds between us.

Although we still pride ourselves on being the furthest you can come from nouveau riche, we had become part of the privileged and affluent, and perhaps had started to act the part more than we acknowledged. Our girls joined the ranks of pretty blonde princesses being led to their £12,000 a year private nursery by someone who was obviously not Mummy. For the first time in my life, I even started to buy business-class airline tickets. It seemed almost natural at the time and we could easily justify the expense. I even took a call from Netjets (the private jet-share company) and thought about it for ten seconds before deciding that it was a serious waste of money.

In Denmark in the late 1970s and early 1980s you were considered wealthy if your family had two cars – which we did. But we were not rich. Not rich like I got to see and experience in London in the early part of the new millennium. As a child I would count my savings every three months. I was so proud when I got to $1,000. Not that I had a target in mind to buy something specific; I just liked the fact that I had the choice of what to do with it, and it was all mine. At around age 12 I got a job delivering newspapers and soon graduated to be a dishwasher in a local restaurant at $5 an hour. Even at the time this was poor pay, but it was great for my quarterly savings calculations as I was quite a stingy kid (this will not come as a surprise to those who know me). Ambition and hunger was already then much more about striving for a target than reaping the tangible fruits of the effort. Odd as it may sound from someone who has spent the majority of his adult life working in finance, the material things were never that important to me.

The chief benefit from our new wealth was more mental than physical. With more money to my name, I felt a new sense of security that things could only go *so* wrong. Gone were the sleepless nights when I feared that Holte would end in miserable failure with me creeping back for food and shelter in my parents' basement. I could afford not to work for a while and still keep up our lifestyle, even if Holte shut down tomorrow. This made life easier and I stopped being constantly on edge. For the first time in a decade, I felt I could relax a little.

From time to time, events would remind me that I did not possess the natural smoothness of someone whose place in the upper classes was secured at birth. One time, at the end of a rare week-long holiday in a pricey suite at the Four Seasons in Sharm El Sheikh, I was presented with a bill to match the annual income of some of my childhood friends. Instead of meticulously checking it, I casually handed over my AmEx to the lady behind the desk.

'I'm sorry, sir. This one has been declined,' she said, embarrassed, after trying it a few times.

'Oh, I have been having problems with it anyway. Just use this one.' I lied back, handing her my Barclaycard.

After five minutes, she came back with a male colleague.

'I am sorry sir. The second card has also been declined. Do you have another one?' She said it quietly, to avoid embarrassing me in front of the queue building up behind me. The last card in my pocket was an ancient Danish bank card that would surely also be declined, so I decided to beat a hasty retreat.

'There must be a mistake somewhere. I'll go and talk to my wife,' I said, trying to leave the impression that this minor inconvenience must have been caused by reckless spousal spending. The lady standing behind me gave a pitying look as I passed her.

And so it was that Puk ended up paying my largest-ever hotel bill with money from her meagre life savings – she called it her stash for when I leave her for a younger woman. So much for being a hotshot hedge-fund manager!

17

Friends and competition

Old-man talk and gossip

In 2006 at the age of 34 I had been in hedge funds for almost a decade and run my own firm for half that time. I was still too young to be a veteran, but because of all the new arrivals from the industry's explosive growth I felt like an old-timer. I found myself making 'old-man comments' like 'back in 1999 the merger arbitrage spreads were so wide you could drive a truck through them' (i.e., the spread between the eventual consideration received in a merger or takeover and the current price of a stock was very large), and generally made remarks to the effect that all these new people coming into the industry didn't know what they were talking about. Excluding of course the possibility that we didn't either! If I had not gone to Harvard Business School or been relatively young myself I would surely have been making those idiotic generalised comments like, 'People from Harvard don't know the first thing about the real world' or 'Young managers don't have the experience to succeed and are there for the taking'.

Over my years roaming the London hedge-fund landscape I made a number of close friends whom I would meet at lunches or conferences. I generally stayed away from the 'idea dinners' or similar things where several funds would collaborate since I felt they were bound to encourage everyone to converge on the same trades. On one occasion, however, I organised a dinner for 8–10 hedge-fund managers in central London. Although it included investors managing double-digit billions of dollars, it was a casual and relaxed affair. Rather than discuss trade ideas, we shared anecdotes

from our experiences or the latest tax scheme, and generally gossiped about
the industry like a group of high-school students. We all knew who was
doing well or poorly and there were plenty of comments like: 'Did you hear
Peter Samson had to shut down?' – said in a 'thank God it wasn't me' tone.
Or more upbeat: 'Did you hear Chris Hohn was up 60 per cent again last
year and paid himself a couple of hundred million dollars?' This was said in
a hopeful 'that could also be me' tone.

Chris Hohn was then the undisputed star of the London hedge-fund
scene. He left Perry Capital (the same Perry who ripped into me early on;
see Chapter 1) in 2003 to set up TCI (The Children's Investment Fund)
through which he would donate a large fraction of the profits to a charity run by his wife, and immediately raised several billion dollars on very
favourable terms. Before he left Perry Capital, he won the European Fund
Manager of the year award, and won it again a couple of times after setting out on his own, despite fierce competition. I had known Chris for
a number of years and knew many people who had worked for him. He
was known to be a tough and demanding boss, although we always had a
friendly relationship. With our offices only a couple of hundred yards apart
in Mayfair we would occasionally bump into each other on the street and I
once went to his office to discuss trades. Shortly before my wife and I had
twins, Chris and his wife had triplets and I joked with him that most of my
investors could only dream of my returns being two thirds of his.

In my ten years in hedge funds I came across a huge number of managers, including perhaps 11–12 of the world's top twenty. As in most
industries, the top guys shared a few common traits. First and fore-
most they were incredibly hungry and driven, and mainly very intelligent
and thoughtful about their work and the world around them. The stere-
otype often described in the press is misleading. Although there were a
few aggressive screamers who would happily stick a fork in your eye to get
ahead, there were also plenty of self-effacing academic types who might
speak less intelligibly than Mr Bean. But in the day-to-day running of Holte
Capital, my interaction with other managers was fairly limited. Like everyone else, we were fully focused on our own issues.

Even if some uninformed commentators pre-2008 gave the impression
that everyone in the hedge-fund world was as successful as Chris Hohn,
that was obviously not the case. Although partners in larger hedge funds
do glean vast wealth every year in management and incentive fees, the stan-

dard hedge-fund fees do not make it a particularly profitable business until you have more than $50 million in assets under management. Just ask my friend who, for the third year, is managing an $11-million fund if he thinks hedge-fund fees are too high and he will tell you that the only things that are too high in his life is his blood pressure and the rent on the apartment he lives in. Over the years I have had many friends who had to close down funds or lose their jobs because of a series of bad returns. But they are like those journeymen athletes who disappear from the scene without anyone noticing that they are gone, until years later you hear about them in some other context. 'Oh yes, I remember him – what happened to him?' would be a typical refrain when you heard that a former hedge-fund analyst had left the industry.

One of the most knowledgeable hedge-fund managers I have come across I met on a two-day tour of a Texas-based shipyard. A company's latest modern semi-submersible rig (the ones that float instead of being fixed to the seabed) was under construction and there was an opportunity to have an informal meeting with the company management. I had done a fair bit of work on the company and its assets and generally felt quite knowledgeable about the oilrig sector, but Ian completely blew me away. The detailed knowledge he had about intricate aspects of the rig and the implications these would have on the company's ability to get contracts around the world was staggering. He knew far more than senior management about the rig market and the company's prospects and, in addition to great technical savvy, showed real market knowledge. I stood next to him, impressed, as he asked the company detailed technical engineering questions and referred back to the drilling engineering course he had taken as part of his study of the company.

Ian was the co-portfolio manager of a fast-growing $800-million fund in New York and as I saw it that was only going one way: up. How unpredictable and harsh the world of hedge funds can be was, however, made clear all too soon. I was surprised and saddened when I heard that Ian's fund was down 60 per cent on the year in 2008 and would start returning money to investors. He was left frustrated and bitter. He had travelled the world and felt that he knew more than the aggregate market in his securities (for once I was inclined to agree), but said that the short-term perspective of his investors left him no room to engage in a random market where there was no saying what stocks would do in the short run. 'It's all a fucking lottery,' he complained – a sentiment that would be endorsed by hundreds of managers in the aftermath of the 2008 meltdown.

Nowhere were you more aware of other hedge-fund managers than at the Versailles-style fundraising conferences held in various beautiful places around the world. On these occasions, you could measure a manager's popularity by the size of the group of people he was talking to at the cocktail parties. The hot manager whose schedule was already filled would often be holding court with a group of potential investors eagerly taking notes, while others would be talking to each other or, worse, nobody.

In my time with Holte Capital I got to experience both extremes. On one occasion, I headed to a conference without a schedule and discovered to my horror that I only had two meetings over the two days I was there. One of those meetings did not turn up for our appointment. My day involved lots of hanging out in my room watching CNN or cornering innocent Morgan Stanley folks who had to talk to me as a client. The following year, by contrast, I had 18 meetings in two days including two large group lunches, and generally felt like Brad Pitt. At one moment, I walked into an elevator where two unfamiliar investors were discussing their frustration at only securing a group meeting later in the day with Holte Capital. How quickly things change. After 20 minutes of the last of my 18 meetings, my brain was completely fried and I could tell the investor I was meeting was also tired after a long day. Instead of struggling through the rest of our hour together, we agreed to go to the bar and have a beer instead. As you might expect, those guys soon became investors.

18

Making your commissions count

Are you being serviced?

Once Holte Capital had grown to a couple of hundred million dollars in assets under management, the world of service providers and financial counterparties started to take note of us. The implication was clear: the more money you had invested, the more fees and attention you got.

As we approached our peak of around $1 billion in invested capital, we were receiving a lot of love from brokers. This was sadly not because of our good looks and charming characters but because of the fees we generated for them. Assuming that we turned over (the hedge-fund term is 'churned') our portfolio 2.5 times in a year we would trade a total volume of $2.5 billion. About 20 per cent of this volume was cheaply traded futures, but the rest was stocks and bonds. As we paid approximately 8 basis points (0.08 per cent) in trade commission, in trading volume alone, we generated about $1.6 million annually in commissions. This is not to say that brokerage is easy money: far from it. It is a fiercely competitive business in which you eat only what you kill and even a near-term failure can get you fired.

> If a medium-sized firm like Holte Capital can generate $1.6 million in trade commissions every year, it becomes obvious why the banks and brokerage houses take you to the Super Bowl.

Yet, if a medium-sized firm like Holte Capital can generate $1.6 million in trade commissions every year, it becomes obvious why the banks and brokerage houses take you to the Super Bowl. Considering that Holte was by no means a large hedge fund, imagine the fierce competition to service and entertain the $10-billion-plus hedge funds.

Annual trading costs	
Invested capital	1,000.0 (in millions)
Churn	2.50X
Annual amount traded	2,500.0 (in millions)
Futures	20%
Non-futures amount	2,000.0
Trading costs	0.08%
Annual commissions	1.60 (in millions)

With the additional money brokers can make from knowing the trade flows, market-making activity, swap-contract fees, stock-loan fees, dividend-enhancement trades, and so on, it all adds up to a tidy amount from Holte alone. With higher assets under management and the promise of greater volume to trade, we were also able to reduce our commission rates.

The commission dollars did not bring us into the big leagues of massive hot IPO (initial public offering) allocations or calls about the development of new technologies from Mary Meeker, but in our little world they made a big difference. We could now call analysts from all the research houses and expect to have them walk us through their analysis and discuss companies or industries for hours. Often you would hear the analyst looking you up on the internal system before committing to talk to you.

In the early days, I often encountered analysts saying, 'Actually, I have another call, but will call you back'. Right. Or, more honestly, 'I am sorry, but our database here says you are not a big enough client for me to be talking to you. Can I put you through to one of our sales people?' Some research analysts had clearly mastered the art of turning you down, while others left a self-important hedge-fund manager feeling rejected and angry.

The game of how to get the most benefit from your commission dollars was also played at the large conferences. Every year Morgan Stanley held a very large TMT (telecom, media and technology) conference at the aptly named Hotel Arts in Barcelona. The hotel's large underground conference centre allowed six simultaneous large company presentations and still left plenty of space for administration, press, computer stations and eating facilities. It was the perfect venue. Companies met investors, journalists, investment bankers and each other. Investors gossipped about the latest rumours or tried to corner well-regarded analysts. Brokers handed out business cards and planned drinks for later. There were men in suits everywhere: in the conference centre, rooms, hallways, gym, restaurants, toilets, marina, outside the hotel in the taxi queue or just standing around having a smoke. Everywhere. Everyone was an unashamed capitalist trying to get ahead. Was this what Karl Marx had seen when he woke up in a cold sweat from his nightmares to write *Das Kapital*?

Although the crowd varied from year to year depending on boom and bust in the technology industry, there were always people trying to get those coveted one-on-one meetings with the hottest companies. Failing that, they would have to make do with being one of five or six investors meeting management teams in the hotel rooms. If the CEO of Nokia was making a presentation at the conference he would typically spend the remainder of the day in one-on-one or small group meetings that Morgan Stanley had set up for him, called 'breakout sessions'. Essentially this was a freebie for Morgan as Morgan could expect to be amply rewarded by their clients in future commission for giving them access to company management, even though it was a two-way system which enabled companies to meet the best potential investors.

Needless to say, if Fidelity asked for a meeting, they would get one, as would any large mutual fund or hedge fund that generated many millions of dollars for Morgan in annual commissions. The rest of us were left fighting for one-to-ones with smaller, less popular companies or for group meetings with slightly larger ones. Sometimes watching the 45-minute presentations downstairs almost signalled, 'I am not important enough to get a one-on-one'. One of my good friends, Henrik, was the telecoms analyst at Fidelity and we would often compare schedules and have a good laugh. His would read like a 'who's who' of telecoms while mine was more like 'who's that?' for the few slots that were even filled. Oliver, my sales representative at Morgan, was brilliant at making a barren schedule sound good: 'I couldn't get you Vodafone – nobody got that – but I managed a 30-minute small group meeting with the CFO of Telefonica Moviles.'

In the meetings with management teams, both at the conferences and elsewhere, our larger size was obviously helpful. If we managed to see company management while we were still a $5 million hedge fund, we would ruin any credibility with them if we had admitted that we would be highly unlikely to have more than a $300,000 position in the company. That would not even be worth the time of the third assistant investor relations manager. Instead we would say, 'We don't disclose the size of the fund, but we would be happy to have someone at Merrill Lynch vouch for us if that would help', knowing full well that we could get a broker there to do this without disclosing our size. Not that the companies would ever check – they would often depend on the investment banks to decide who was important enough to meet, and once in the meeting mainly cared about the quality of questions or the level of research done by potential investors. As Holte Capital grew, we would still aim to get maximum clout without ever lying. We would say stuff like, 'We don't like to disclose our size, but we need to be able to have at least a $10 million investment and are not afraid to have stakes large enough that we have to disclose them to the authorities', knowing that this could mean that we might be just a $100 million fund, but could just as easily be a $10 billion one.

Fun and games

The added commission also provided welcome light relief in the form of fun invitations from brokers. They would often invite us to sports events or dinners hoping that, over time, this would result in greater trading activity. All other things being equal, who would not rather make a trade with a guy you knew and liked than one you didn't? We agreed that whenever a goodie like this was offered by a broker, we should send someone from Holte to deepen our relationship – so that there would actually be a business reason behind all the fun. But, depending on the event, we all found great reasons why we could benefit from going to something. Brian decided that going to the Formula 1 Grand Prix in Monaco with Credit Suisse was a great opportunity for him to 'see what they were really like', as we were in the early stages of deciding on another prime broker. The fact he liked them a lot personally and was bound to have a great time may have played a small role in his decision!

A month later, when Brian had secured tickets to an all-important football match, I called Mark, a friend from one of our largest investors, and asked him for a favour. 'Could you call up Brian,' I said conspiratorially, 'and say your CEO is in town from New York and that he wants an opera-tional due-diligence meeting with Holte which, unfortunately, he can only do tonight around 7:30?' I explained that Brian had been bragging about his football tickets all day and I wanted to wind him up.

A minute later, the phone rang in Brian's glass office. I tried hard not to crack up as I saw him close his eyes and slowly shake his head while his shoulders dropped. After he hung up the phone, he dropped his head on his desk and stayed like that for a minute or so, his dreams crushed. Unable to stop myself any longer, I went to his office and asked as innocently as I could, 'Is everything OK? You seem a little down.'

'You won't believe it,' said Brian. 'Mark just insisted on a meeting tonight and they can't do it any other time.' He seemed on the verge of tears, and I couldn't hold my composure any longer. As I burst out laugh-ing, Brian realised it was a wind-up. Childish perhaps, but fun all the same.

The bull market was eerily obvious at the annual rounds of 2005 and 2006 Christmas parties. No expense was spared as nightclubs in Mayfair were rented for the evening and speakers brought in to entertain the half-drunk throng of traders and fill them with luxurious food and drink. I had the celebrity chef Aldo Zilli serve me a bowl of pasta and he signed his book, which I gave to my neighbour for Christmas. There were stand-up comedians, politicians (sometimes hard to tell the difference), explorers and athletes, and while a lot of them had well-rehearsed stories with funny punchlines, you could tell that often they didn't really care about us khaki-clad finance clowns. But there would be a new party every night in December and ski trips in the Alps at weekends. Always finding a reason for going to a party, I enjoyed meeting the brokers and analysts in a more casual setting than faceless conference rooms.

Although I went to conferences where the bar resembled a frat party, I was never offered drugs or knew many who used them. It makes sense – what hedge funds do is highly mentally challenging and you need to be at the top of your game for a long working day to compete. Turning up at work in a drug haze, you would be bound to make costly mistakes and eventually get sacked. Perhaps visiting prostitutes and strip clubs are more obvious sins, and there was a fair bit of that. I have been to a couple of broker parties where there were a large number of women with limited mathematical skills but more obvious physical appeal. Although it was not something we managers would really talk about among ourselves, we were probably never more than a phone call to the right broker away from all of that. I just don't think that many of my hedge-fund friends made those calls very often. But then perhaps I'm am just boring.

Top-end entertainment

One of the better entertainment trips I went on was a golf outing to France. In a group of 12–14 managers, we were taken in a private jet to play at one of the best courses in France, conveniently located in a top wine district. The trip was from Thursday afternoon, returning on Saturday after lunch. Leaving the office I was running late to make the agreed departure time from the private airfield in South London and ended up taking the train there. The paradox of heading to a private jet in a packed Underground train hugging my golf clubs did not evade me, and I managed to be the last one to turn up. I guess I can now forever say, 'I had a private jet wait for me', even if that sounds a lot more posh than it was.

The course was set in a lush green rolling landscape surrounding the beautiful chateau which doubled as clubhouse. After landing we had taken mainly small country lanes directly to the chateau and I was left with a feeling that we had landed on a different planet far away from normal life. As the plane landed, I was still not exactly sure where in France we were other than we had flown approximately 45 minutes after reaching the French coast.

Of course it was brilliant fun. The host had hired a couple of former tour players to play with us, and I played with a guy who had held the halfway lead in a major a couple of decades ago. After playing, a 'trick golfer' did a fantastic array of stunts including hitting balls with a six-foot club and hitting two balls simultaneously (try it – it's harder than it looks). We were then led to a wine-tasting and on to a sumptuous dinner. The following day we played another round before being flown back to London. I asked a guy who managed a very large fund what the next level up of entertainment would be and he shrugged his shoulders.

'Well, you are probably talking about small private dinners with famous artists or heads of state, but I haven't been to anything like that myself.'

My missed £100,000 golf lesson

One of the biggest 'see and be seen' events in Europe was the annual charity dinner for a foundation called 'Absolute Returns for Kids' (ARK). The foundation was started by one of the funds-of-funds heavies, Arpad Busson.

One year the foundation had taken over the massive area around Battersea power station on the south bank of the Thames in London. There was a tent the size of the Superdome divided by a curtain that dropped from 100 feet above to separate the drinks from the dining area. After passing through the tightest security imaginable, I was met by an army of waiters with trays of champagne and fluffy-looking cocktails. Oh, wait. They were all wearing my exact outfit. Years before I had been to a wedding in India and had forgotten to bring my battle-scarred tuxedo. Instead of buying a new one, I thought it fun at the time to buy an Indian-style Nehru suit and wear that instead. As my waistline expanded, I outgrew my tuxedo and came to view the Nehru suit as my *de facto* formal wear. What I had not counted on was the increasing prevalence of that same suit as a waiter's outfit in bars and restaurants. I know now, thank you. Anyway, back to the ARK dinner and 15 requests from other hedge-fund guys to get them a glass of champagne. Even Elle Macpherson commented on my outfit when I was briefly introduced to her. How cool is that? A fashion icon commenting on my outfit! Even if it was to say that I looked like a waiter.

Unlike the more exclusive crowd at Versailles, I actually knew tons of people already at my first ARK dinner. Some were people I had gone to university with, some I knew from my time at HBK and some I had met after starting out on my own. I had an oddly comforting feeling of belonging in the crowd. Since we were out of our office uniform, it somehow felt right to talk about things other than investment performance. Even my competitors seemed almost like friends with a glass of champagne in hand.

The curtain separating the two halves of the massive tent dropped dramatically to reveal an opulent dining area where the see-through half of the tent showed the power station lit up by enormous lights, Gotham City style. A wire extended from the top of the power station high above the dining area and a young woman slid down to the auctioneer's chair to launch the evening's festivities. It all seemed to say: 'Welcome to the big time.'

As the guest of a bank we had considered as a second prime broker, I sat at their table next to David Philips who, soon after, took his hedge-fund public in a billion-dollar IPO. A celebrity was the auctioneer. This was the time for the big players to announce their presence on the scene. Middle-management types were not going to outbid them for the glamorous prizes and their moment in the spotlight.

Before the Monopoly money started being thrown around, a young woman came on stage and spoke passionately about the good deeds that came from the money that nights like tonight made possible. She was not funny or famous, only dead serious about her work, and she seemed a stark reminder to this tough crowd that money alone has no purpose: it's what you do with it that counts.

I am probably an intellectual snob who acts hard to impress, but these auction lots were impressive. You could bid for a day playing tennis with Tony Blair at Chequers (the PM's country residence), have Tom Ford design a dress especially for you (he was there for the evening), have Gordon Ramsay cook a meal in your home, play football with Ronaldo, or sail on Roman Abramovich's yacht, as well as the almost obligatory private-jet trips to private islands and so on. I kept expecting them to say, 'And our next lot is the Fountain of Youth', but it was not to be. Most of the lots went for between £100,000 and £150,000. With a couple of hundred people in the crowd, it was hard to see who was bidding, and I certainly kept my hands in my pockets lest scratching my nose be mistaken for a bid. I had yet to buy a sofa for our new place and Puk would probably not have been impressed if I had paid £100,000 to have Colin Montgomerie work on my backswing for an hour.

Are we worth it?

An expensive acquaintance

In early 2006, I was at the wedding of a good friend in the home town of his bride outside Chicago. At the reception I sat next to the bride's charming aunt, Mrs Straw. Mrs Straw had lived in the small town all her life and her husband was a couple of years from retiring from the local sub-supplier for one of the Detroit auto companies. She had not worked for a decade. Soon the conversation turned to what I did for a living.

'I work at an investment management company,' I said.

'Oh, interesting. Like a mutual fund?' she asked.

'Sort of. It's called a hedge fund but it is quite similar in many ways.'

'I know what a hedge fund is,' she said, slightly offended that I had assumed she would not. 'We're invested in them through my husband's pension plan at the plant. They're great. He is so close to retiring and the pension manager told the folks that hedge funds were like a guarantee against markets going down.'

'Sort of like a sure thing,' I suggested. 'Which funds are you invested with?'

'I think they invest in a couple of what are called funds of funds who are then able to pick the best hedge funds,' she said.

'That's great,' I said, before moving the conversation on to other things.

The brother of the groom, who had given up investment banking earlier that year, had observed our conversation from across the table. 'Dude,' he said later, 'everyone's in hedge funds these days. It's the way of saying "I am a sophisticated investor" even if many people don't have a clue what hedge funds actually do.'

The following morning, as I was waiting for Puk to get ready for the post-wedding brunch, I absentmindedly jotted down some figures on the notepad by the bed while watching some basketball highlights. These were numbers I had known about for a long time, but never really focused on or added up from the perspective of the ultimate end investor. They went like this: pension-fund adviser 0.25 per cent, pension-fund fees and expenses 0.75 per cent, fund-of-funds management fee 1 per cent, and so on.

> These were numbers I had known about for a long time, but never really focused on or added up from the perspective of the ultimate end investor.

'There are a lot of people who need to get paid here before my friends from last night see a penny,' I thought, increasingly aware of the staggering aggregation of fees. I would cross out many of the fee levels and make them lower so that the aggregate fees would be more reasonable.

'Surely external pension fund advisers only charge 0.15 per cent per year,' I would mutter to myself.

Still, my conclusions were troubling, and I began to think the only way the numbers made sense for them would be if the hedge funds all performed brilliantly every year – which clearly wasn't the case. Typically, Mr Straw's pension fund would have its own set of expenses and fees on top of the external adviser often hired to assess what to do with the hedge-fund allocation. With the help of this adviser, Mr Straw's pension fund would typically make an allocation to one or more of the larger funds of funds, depending on their risk appetite and their views on which fund of funds showed greatest promise. The fund of funds selected would then go about its work and decide which hedge fund to invest in, including funds like Holte Capital. That is a lot of mouths to feed, particularly when you consider that the hedge funds, on top of their typical fees, have expenses associated with trading and administration. Below is a summary of all the annual fees and expenses Mr Straw could incur before seeing a return from his hedge-fund investment:

Pension fund (PF)	Fees Recurring (%)	If profit (%)	
PF external adviser	0.15		
PF fees & expenses	0.75		
Fund of funds (FoF)			
FoF expenses	0.15		Administration, legal, audit, etc.
FoF management fee	1.00		
FoF performance fee		10.00	
Hedge fund (HF)			
HF trading expenses	1.64		See below
HF fund expenses	0.20		Administration, legal, audit, etc.
HF management fee	1.50		
HF performance fee		20.00	

Note that in this zero interest rate environment Mr Straw is down more than 5 per cent (before incentive fees) on his investment every year on fixed costs alone. He would be well advised to question if the hedge-fund investment business can consistently provide opportunities to justify this.

Trading expenses clearly depend on the type of hedge fund. In this case I assumed a typical long/short equity fund with 150 per cent long and 75 per cent short exposure – somewhat different from Holte Capital which aimed to be more equally long and short, although the math is fairly similar for other types of funds. In order to generate its investment returns this fund will typically incur trading expenses as summarised below.

Breakdown of hedge-fund trading expenses		
Long market value	150.00%	Long $150 per $100 in assets
Short market value	75.00%	Short $75 per $100 in assets
Borrow fee	0.50%	Can be higher for hard-to-borrow names
Annual churn	2.50×	Number of times portfolio traded yearly
Bid/offer spread	0.25%	Bigger for small names
Commissions	0.10%	In the USA this is done in cents/share
Softing	0.00%	Assumes none
Margin costs	0.00%	Assumed zero as below 100% net long
Borrow fee	0.38%	
Commissions	0.56%	Gross market value × churn × commissions
Bid/offer spread	0.70%	Gross market value × churn × bid/offer × 0.5
Total	1.64%	

At Holte Capital our administrative expenses were under 0.2 per cent per year, but for smaller funds, this figure could easily be several per cent annually. Even adding the 0.2 per cent to trading expenses listed above, the fund has spent nearly 2 per cent (0.2% + 1.64%) of its assets yearly before the hedge-fund manager gets his management fee. And the list goes on. In some cases, at least until a couple of years ago, hedge-fund managers also engaged in 'softing'. This is when a broker charges you more than the going rate for at trade (say 0.2 per cent instead of 0.1 per cent) and gives part of this difference back to you in the form of things like a Bloomberg terminal, computers, etc. This effectively makes the hedge fund charge its investors higher fees. In line with Holte Capital, this example assumes there is no 'softing' going on (as if we did not charge people enough already!).

But back to Mr Straw's pension. Let us for simplicity's sake assume that all the hedge-fund managers the fund of funds had invested in returned 10 per cent before any fees and trading and other expenses. How much does Mr Straw get to bring home to Mrs Straw to help them enjoy their golden years? Not a lot, as it turns out. In the table below, you can see that in this simple example Mr Straw gets around 3 per cent return per year even as the hedge-fund managers do quite respectably with a 10 per cent gross return. Hold that thought. Every time Mr Straw's money generated a return of $10, he got to keep less than $3.

Heaven forbid that Mr Straw would have to pay tax on his gains. Instead of enriching the many layers of financial advisers and principals, Mr Straw should just have put his money in Treasury bonds, and slept easily at night (particularly as his retirement date was fast approaching) or a stock-market index fund if he wanted market exposure. But wouldn't Mr Straw be quite upset with the company canteen folks if they forced him to pay this kind of price premium for a slightly more exotic-sounding and -tasting fruit as part of his standard company lunch?

The example described needs one further explanation. Namely, how did the hedge fund generate its 10 per cent return? If the hedge fund was just long the Standard & Poor's 500 index and that index was up 10 per cent for the year, Mr Straw would have paid large fees for very little additional value. He could just have bought a Vanguard index fund and paid 0.2 per cent in total fees, not 7 per cent (although he might not be able to avoid some pension-fund costs to gain tax advantages). The directional funds still charge the fees, but do not add as much value (they just own something

'Gross' gross performance*		10.00%
	Fee:	Net of:
Hedge fund		
HF trading expenses	1.64%	8.36%
Standard quoted gross performance*		**8.36%**
HF fund expenses	0.20%	8.16%
HF management fee	1.50%	6.66%
HF incentive fee	20.00%	5.33%
Fund of funds		
FoF expenses	0.15%	5.18%
FoF management fee	1.00%	4.18%
FoF incentive fee	10.00%	3.76%
Pension fund		
PF external adviser	0.15%	3.61%
PF fees & expenses	0.75%	2.86%
Net return		**2.86%**

*Normally gross performance is quoted after trading expenses

that went up) as those with 10 per cent pure alpha (value generation) – more on this later. As the events of the fall of 2008 suggest, a large number of hedge funds are indeed long the markets and the value they generate was thus lower. Investors were paying for beta – paying for being long the market, rather than true alpha. It is no coincidence that the growth surge in hedge-fund assets occurred at the same time as a historic bull-market run in equities and other asset classes. There has been a lot of beta (market exposure) sold as alpha, yet how much is perhaps not readily apparent to the end-investor until the market starts going down, and even then there are ways to disguise it.

Speaking from personal experience, it is incredibly hard to generate 10 per cent gross 'alpha' every year. If you did, funds of funds would love you and invest lots of money with you and simply gear their investment in your fund to fit their risk profile. The holy grail of funds-of-funds investing is to create a portfolio of hedge funds with no correlation to markets or each other, thus almost guaranteeing continued positive performance. Unfortunately there is very little doubt that we as an industry don't create an average of 10 per cent alpha per year; we create far less and correlate quite highly with each other, particularly in bad markets. In the good years healthily rising markets might disguise the fact that it is not 10 per cent alpha, but rather 3 per cent alpha and 7 per cent being long the market that generated the returns. Mr Straw may not know the difference and happily pay his fees. But in the long run the fees will undoubtedly catch up with Mr Straw and the hedge-fund industry and reveal that it is not generating nearly enough value for the fees it charges. Something will have to give: the hedge-fund industry will either have to start charging lower fees, generally decline in size, or only charge fees when it can demonstrate actual outperformance. As the fallout from the turmoil of 2008 shows, there seems to be a good deal of evidence of at least the first two points.

To get an idea of the scale of fees, imagine Mr Straw invested $100 in the type of fund used in the example above, while Mrs Straw takes $100 from her savings and puts it in a Vanguard fund. Now suppose that both those investments return 10 per cent per year before any fees over the ten-year period of the investment until Mr and Mrs Straw are ready for retirement. The results are both obvious and staggering.

	Year 0	Year 10
Mr Straw in 'Hot Hedge'	$100.00	$132.57
Mrs Straw in Vanguard	$100.00	$254.70
Cumulative fees to 'Hot Hedge'		$35.48
Cumulative fees to fund of funds		$17.76
Cumulative fees to Vanguard*		$4.68

* at 0.2% per year

A simplistic example, but the fees to the hedge fund and fund of funds are ten times higher than those to Vanguard, and this is before pension-fund costs, expenses or trading costs. This does not mean that hedge funds are never the best option, but rather that the bar Mr Straw has to clear for it to make sense for him to have money with a hedge fund is very high indeed.

I was still working through this when Puk was finally ready to head out for the wedding brunch. As we took the short walk down the street to the aunt's house, I tried to explain my rediscovered revelation about the multiple fee structure and how it probably did not make sense for Mr and Mrs Straw or even pension funds generally to be invested in hedge funds, but Puk was oddly casual about it. 'Don't you think the rest of the world knows that finance guys are not worth what they are getting paid?' she said with a smile before continuing, 'And are you and Holte not a part of the problem rather than the solution?' I gave Puk the usual song and dance about uncorrelated risk-adjusted returns at Holte Capital, but her mind was already elsewhere.

PART FOUR

The fast road down

20

Feeling grim

Burnt out

'A stroll after the close? There's something I want to chat with you about.' The email from Brian was nothing unusual. We would often go down to Grosvenor Square to have a chat in the fresh air, where the team wouldn't see us. At that point we had been running Holte Capital together for four years, me as the portfolio manager and Brian as the CFO. We had had our ups and downs, but I felt our friendship was stronger for it, and I felt incredibly lucky to have Brian working with me.

On the short walk down Brook Street we made a point of never discussing confidential business issues. Mayfair was swarming with hedge-fund people but Grosvenor Square with its open layout further down the street was a place where we could talk without worrying about being overheard.

'I'm sorry to spring this on you,' said Brian, 'but I've decided it's time for me to call it a day.'

I just looked him in stunned silence.

'I've thought a lot about it over the past months and the more I think about it the more I'm sure that I just don't have it in me any more.'

'Oh shit,' I said.

'Yeah, I am really sorry,' said Brian, 'but you're the first to know. And don't worry – I'm not going somewhere else. In fact, I have no plans other than to take some time away from it all and travel. And to be honest, from what we have been talking about for the past few years, you should think about it too.'

Like anyone in a stressful job, Brian and I would often go to the pub and complain about how the constant demand for performance was taking its toll on us. Holte Capital had come from next to nothing and been a relative success, yet neither of us seemed able to savour it. Instead, there always seemed to be another make-or-break moment. The previous couple of months had been particularly stressful, and our complaints had magnified.

Once I had had a chance to compose myself and get over the shock of Brian's resignation, it was clear where this was going.

'You sound like this isn't about money, and that you have pretty much made up your mind,' I said. 'As a friend I understand you, but as a business partner I find it hard.'

Brian assured me that he would stay as long as I needed him to. We discussed how this was the kind of business where there never seemed like a good time to walk away, and Brian felt that people who dared to make dramatic changes in their life more often turned out to be happy that they chose change over complacency.

After we had looped the square so often that the security personnel at the US embassy had started to take notice of us (and probably updated our FBI file), I was more confused than ever. Until Brian quit, I had never seriously thought of closing Holte Capital, but his decision to walk away suddenly made it seem like an option worth considering.

I took the next couple of days off to think about Brian's decision and ponder whether I should join him on the sidelines. These were the main pros and cons as I saw them:

> Until Brian quit, I had never seriously thought of closing Holte Capital, but his decision to walk away suddenly made it seem like an option worth considering.

Reasons for quitting

■ **You don't need the money.** Although many people in hedge funds had made a lot more than my double-digit million investment in Holte, it was still plenty for my purposes – especially as I had no expensive habits. I had always assumed that once I no longer needed the money I would enjoy the work more. But it hadn't worked out that way. Instead I found myself increasingly questioning how much I actually liked the work or found it meaningful.

■ **This bubble has to burst.** This was 2006 and London and the financial industry felt like a massive bubble. So many people were making and raising silly amounts of money as if they were dancing the night away on board the Titanic. A decent family home in central London often started at $7–8 million and we were paying as much for my twins to go to nursery school for four hours a day as I had paid to go to Harvard. Maybe now was a good time to walk away? Was this what San Francisco had felt like in 1999?

■ **You are not changing the world.** I had always wanted to do something that would make the world a better place. Not necessarily feed the poor, but at least make a positive impact. Although I could argue to anyone at a dinner party that creating alpha at a hedge fund added value, we were not trying to find or develop the next eBay, inventing better ways of reducing pollution, or writing the next great novel.

■ **Markets can't be beaten after fees.** We had tried as hard as we could with the best resources available in the market, and I genuinely thought the quality of our work was as high as I have seen anywhere in the industry. That said, I was starting to doubt whether we as an industry and perhaps even Holte individually could beat the markets consistently, net of fees. Since we would charge over 5 per cent per year (expenses + management fee + incentive fee) the hurdle might just be too big and the markets too efficient.

■ **What about family life?** For the first three years of their lives, I rarely saw my twin girls from Sunday night to Saturday morning. I left before they got up and returned home after they went to bed. Although I thought my marriage was good, being a hedge-fund manager was clearly detrimental to a happy family life. But then isn't that the sob story you hear from all high-powered executives before they divorce for the third time and go back to work?

Reasons for carrying on

■ **Count your blessings.** Where else could you make about $4 million a year? Why walk away from that kind of money when you are still 34 years old? The job may not be nirvana, but you are making bundles and whose job is that fantastic anyway? Stop whining and get back to your desk!

■ **It's fun running your own show.** Ever since high school, when I had arranged ski tours from Denmark to the Alps and sold winter clothing as part of my own little business, I had always wanted to be an entrepreneur. With Holte Capital, I had actually started a business that had gone on to be highly profitable, and this was something I was proud to have done. It had done well in the face of great adversity, and to give up just because I was feeling a bit burnt out felt weak.

■ **What about the stakeholders?** There were six people working for me, all of whom I really liked and to whom I felt a tremendous responsibility. After all, they had shown faith in me by coming to work at Holte. I also liked our investors and thought they were far more thoughtful and imaginative than the average hedge-fund investor. I did not want to let them down.

■ **Market-neutral investing does add value**. If you are genuinely market-neutral, you provide your investors with a valuable product. This was what we were trying to do and I at least thought it was an honest proposition.

■ **At last the risk profile is about right.** After being far too low-risk since its inception, Holte Capital was finally at the risk levels it should be and this would either make the fund succeed or fail in short order. As I really did enjoy most of the work and thought our trades and analysis added a lot of value, the validation that the higher risk could bring would surely feel fantastic.

■ **What else would you do?** I did not have something else I was burning to do, other than to take a long holiday. Since business school I had been toying with a very low-cost, multiple index-fund product, but I was far from ready to start that now. Then again, not knowing what else to do didn't make it right to carry on.

There was no doubt that I was burnt out and my doubts about the industry and the work were coming to the fore. I had long chats with Puk about it and although she said she would support me whichever decision I made, she also said it was clear that I was not happy with my work or health.

In the end I decided to stay with the business and recruit a CFO to replace Brian. Brian stuck to his promise and ended up staying six months while I found his replacement. But his leaving was a massive wake-up call for me and I tried to adjust my priorities. I tried to start exercising more and joined a gym. I tried to leave earlier in the evening when there was less to do, committed to taking more holidays, and so on. But soon it was back to business as usual and my commitment to introspection and 'better life' was replaced by the daily grind of chasing returns for our investors.

Francois joined us as Brian's replacement in November of 2006 just in time to see out a good overall 2006 and start 2007 on an upbeat note. We were up just under 15 per cent net to the investors for the year and had achieved that with little obvious correlation to the markets. Also our risk levels were now up to a level where we could hope to have that kind of return every year, regardless of the markets. Things were looking good.

Shorting a 'good' company

Hedge funds are often derided in the press and elsewhere as being unscrupulous vultures that prey on the weak and take their pound of flesh regardless of the impact this has on the world around them. Although this is a gross simplification of an often thoughtful and complex group of individuals, it is true that we sometimes trade in a way that leaves a bad taste in the mouth.

Our short position in German-based Fresenius was an example of a trade that gave me moral scruples. While undoubtedly as profit-hungry a company as any listed business, Fresenius profited by doing good in the world. The company consisted of four business units: Fresenius Medical Care (FMC), which was a New York-listed leader in products for chronic kidney failure, Fresenius Kabi, a leader in infusion therapy, Biotech, which did antibody research, and a unit that provided specialised hospital management. Fresenius had a majority stake in FMC and the rest of the company was quoted on the stock exchange. The basis for our trade was fairly simple. If you deconsolidated the financial statements of Fresenius so that they excluded FMC (also taking out their debt), you could recreate effective stand-alone financial statements for Fresenius ex-FMC. You could then compare this with the market value of Fresenius once you deducted the value of their stake in FMC. And this part of the overall Fresenius was trading far too high. Fresenius was controlled by a foundation that would never sell the business and the company should therefore not trade at any kind of potential takeover premium. In our view it was an interesting and good mid-sized European medical company that was trading much too expensively. So we shorted the stock and bought shares in FMC to effectively recreate a short position in Fresenius ex-FMC – a typical hedge-fund trade.

I often thought of Fresenius as the kind of company you wouldn't want to be a client of unless you really had to. If you were using Fresenius Kabi's products it might be because you were mortally ill or had been in a traffic accident and you were unable to absorb nutrients in a normal way and had to use their sophisticated intravenous systems. A client of the biotech unit might recently have received an organ transplant and need the products to help prevent an organ rejection. And finally a client in the hospital management business would be there because of Fresenius's expertise in acute treatment and rehabilitation. To these clients Fresenius's ability to develop new products and treatments often meant the difference between life and death. And at Holte Capital we were short the company and would profit from its decline and failure.

I could see myself walking down a corridor next to a tall man in a white coat. The sun was shining through the large panoramic windows to our right. The man next to me had the stern and tired expression of someone who had spent a lifetime giving bad news and he was slightly hunched over as if the weight of the world was on his shoulders. His mouth was open and he was talking to me, but I could not make out the words. Slowly I came to. He was talking about my brother and he was angry.

'We would have found a cure,' he said. 'There wasn't enough money to complete the project. They would have raised money in the stock market but someone had sold the stock down to the point where management gave up the idea and abandoned the project. I am sorry.'

Wait. What is he talking about? We kept walking and his words became indecipherable again. We came to the end of the hallway and I saw my brother sitting in a wheelchair under a sign that said Fresenius Research Facility. He looked up at me and said: 'Don't worry Lars – you did what you had to do.'

Then he surrendered to the spasms . . .

I woke up trying to catch my breath. My T-shirt was wet with sweat. I got out of bed to take a shower. It was already 5am and the early morning light signalled the start of a new day. There was no point in going back to bed. With my eyes closed under the hot water in the shower I felt angry with myself.

'Why do you have such stupid dreams? It is not how the real world works. In the real world people try to make money. Besides, Fresenius does not do multiple sclerosis research at all.' I was in complete denial that there might be anything wrong with my world.

In a movie, I would have gone back to work that morning, unwound the Fresenius trade and donated the profits from it to a charity. But I didn't. There was money to be made.

21

A bad day

The start of a bad day

The day started like most other days. I walked through the park on my way to work, making sure to not walk too fast or I would break into a sweat on this hot August morning in 2007. Things had not been going too well at Holte Capital. We were flat for the year to the end of July as many trades had not worked out. Not a catastrophe, but after four conservative up years I wanted to step up a gear, and we didn't seem able to.

I arrived at Brook Street at my usual hour of 7.15, with an espresso in hand, walked past the security guard and up the three flights of stairs to our beautiful, light office. Mildly annoyed that I was the first one there, I logged on to my computer via the centre of my three-screen set-up.

The subject line of the first email was enough. 'Aker Yards Profit Warning . . . bad', it said. My heart sank. Shit. How bad? Please, not too bad. The news had just hit the tape and the headlines were coming in on my Bloomberg terminal as I opened the press release the company had sent out.

It was bad. Really bad.

Aker Yards is a Norwegian-based company with operations across the world, but with a focus on Europe. The company had three major business units: construction of cruise vessels, specialised vessels (such as submarine construction vessels), and 'other' vessels, including Arctic vessels. We had done extensive work on the company and I was about to go to Finland to visit two of the yards. In our view Aker Yards was a ripe takeover candidate and was trading far too cheap relative to a group of its peers (in Asia) that did not have the benefit of its diversified product base and market-leading position in the growing cruise sector, and had much greater exposure to the construction of more commoditised types of vessels. In a downturn Aker Yards would be much better positioned with its more advanced technology and there was no cost disadvantage as labour-intensive production was carried out in low-cost countries. At half the multiples of the Asian competitors – despite a generally more stable growth profile – we thought it a great opportunity. In our trade we were long Aker Yards and hedged the trade with a mix of its Asian competitors and some of the cruise operators. We were trying to capture as purely as possible the cheapness of Aker Yards and its takeover potential (the company was in fact bought a year later – too late). We were not making a bet on the cruise or offshore cycle. That was not our game.

The press release made depressing reading. There were unforeseen cost overruns at a shipyard in Finland and the company did not seem clear on their extent or impact. As usual, the management promised a 'thorough review of operations' and said they would 'implement the necessary measures'. What else were they going to do?

As the other analysts spilled into the office, I was urgently re-reading the release, trying to find out more about the order book at the specific yard, trying to talk to the brokers, who did not know anything else, or trying to get through to my contact at the company. All at once. As in most of our trades, we had tried to get an inside scoop by getting someone closer to the yards to tell us how things were going. 'Really smoothly', said our source. At that moment I wanted to hit him with something hard.

Right from the opening of the markets, Aker Yards plummeted. From a price of around 100 Norwegian kroner per share, the price quickly declined to 80 and down further from there. We were down a million dollars. No, wait. Two million. Three, four. A jump down. Six, seven. Fuck me. This is a big one.

We had a large position in the stock and although my first reaction was that the fall was exaggerated, we did not want to add to the position before we had more information. Also, we already had such a large exposure that adding would have been an irresponsible thing to do. The cemetery of hedge-fund collapses is filled with investors who bought in again when they thought things could not get worse. Because we had spent so much time talking to management over the past couple of months we got through to

them as one of the first investors. They
were already on their way to London
to lunch with investors to explain the
situation. I was slightly worried that management felt that this was a serious enough
situation that they had to drop everything
and fly to London to reassure investors.

> The cemetery of hedge-
> fund collapses is filled with
> investors who bought in
> again when they thought
> things could not get worse.

The stock dropped further to the mid-
70s and I was quickly running out of people to talk to. We were down
about $10 million on the day – this was going to be more than just a really
bad day. This could shorten the life of Holte Capital.

I had already talked to all the research analysts who covered the stock,
brokers, and the few competitors I could get through to. I had this odd
sense that there must be more I could do, but had a hard time concen-
trating, as my eyes kept flicking back to the market screen for Aker Yards.
Every second the stock seemed to tick down, costing us more and more. I
wanted to say 'STOP. Please stop. Can't we just all not look at this right
now and return to it in six months when they have had a chance to correct
the mess?' I wanted to run out of the office and escape to the nearest coffee
shop so that I would not have to stare into the abyss. Perhaps it would be
better when I got back? But obviously I could not abandon ship in the
middle of a crisis in which the market would move wildly after every real or
perceived piece of news from Aker Yards. Watching the stock tick down was
like dying by a thousand cuts.

By mid-morning it was clear that this was going to be our worst day
ever. We would be down around 3 per cent of the fund unless management
somehow managed to convince everyone at lunch that this was all a bad
joke and that the company was actually facing an imminent takeover at a
large premium. That was unlikely.

It was an odd relief to take the Central line to St Paul's station for the
lunch meeting. The train was much faster than a taxi in the midday traffic and the Underground ride meant 20 minutes without phone reception
and more bad news. The lunch was held at the corporate offices of Enskilda
Banken – a Nordic bank – with fantastic views of St Paul's Cathedral below.
Not that any of the 25 or so participants seemed to care. Before the meeting
started all the guests stood around in the reception area trying to look casual.
I bumped into an old friend who at least was honest enough to admit that

he was bleeding. 'Those bastard fuckers' was his summary of the situation. Others tried to look as if they might be here for the lunch but that does not mean that they were stupid enough to lose money on the situation. I normally dislike such people. On 'Aker Yards' day I despised them.

Management turned up and everyone followed them into the conference room. They were clearly not happy about the situation and quickly abandoned the presentation they had brought. Nobody wanted to talk about the damned second quarter. Several people asked: How could this have happened? How can we trust you again? Tell us again how your 'best of breed' internal controls failed to spot this? And so on. Even the waiters serving lunch seemed to pause as one particularly irate investor vented his anger and suggested that management resign. Management seemed almost frustratingly unruffled and kept explaining how the delays and cost overruns at a large Finnish yard had been completely unforeseeable. Instead of their cool demeanour, you almost wanted them to start crying or at least show some pain at realising how many millions their announcement had cost the assembled lunch group and wider shareholder base.

Back in the office I was trying to go over the numbers again to measure the impact that the delays and cost overruns would have on the margins of the business, but could not stop myself looking at the trading screen. More losses. 'Surely they are not going to go bankrupt?' I thought as the stock went down 30 per cent.

A bad day gets worse

My miserable day quickly took a turn for the worse. Our office manager Doriana came over to my desk with a worried expression as I was on the phone with yet another research analyst, and she was clearly intent on getting my attention. 'Someone named Miss Karen from Strawberry Fields Nursery is on the phone. It is about one of your daughters. She said it was urgent.' Anyone who has been on the receiving end of that kind of a phone call can imagine what went through my head in the five seconds before I picked up the call. Please. Please. Please. Let them not be hurt. The field of play completely cleared that instant and Aker Yards immediately became insignificant. Something far more important might be going on.

If Strawberry Fields needed to get in touch with us they would simply call our nanny, Febe, or my wife. That they would call me at work could

only mean bad news. In the short history of Holte Capital this might have
been a defining moment. In the middle of an investment meltdown it was
a stark reminder that I had something at home that I cared about infinitely
more than the performance of Holte Capital.

'Mr Kroijer? It's Karen from Strawberry Fields. I think you'd better
come to the nursery and pick up Anna. She's got a piece of metal stuck in
her eye that we can't get out. You need to take her to the eye hospital.'

'Oh no,' I thought and stupidly asked, 'Is she OK?' I couldn't think of
anything more intelligent to say. She had been playing with some of the
other kids and somehow got some metal stuck in her eye. She had cried a
lot and then fallen asleep. They had tried to ring both our nanny and my
wife, but been unable to get through to either. On this 'one in a thousand'
kind of day it somehow made sense that they had both left their mobile
phones at home before going out. I thanked Karen for getting in touch
with me, got up from my desk and told the team to contact me if there
were any developments in the Aker Yards situation.

Absurd as it sounds, I was really relieved. Strawberry Fields is a top
London nursery and had there been anything seriously wrong with Anna
they would not have hesitated in calling an ambulance. In the seconds
before I knew the story, I had feared far worse.

In the taxi going to the nursery in Notting Hill I felt ashamed at my
relief at escaping from the office. I was glad that I had an excuse to leave
the office and avoid the grim reality of the Aker Yards situation. There were
many things I could have done to improve our understanding of the new
situation and be better prepared for what undoubtedly would be highly volatile trading sessions in the days ahead. I could have gone to Finland and
tried to see the yard manager, or pored over the accounts and presentations
for the umpteenth time. Instead, I was relieved that I could be out of the
office with a good conscience and focus on something else, something most
people undoubtedly would consider more important. 'It's just money',
people who have never worked in finance might say. 'It's never just money',
people in finance might answer.

The taxi arrived at Kensington Park Road and I rushed into the nursery after passing through the Fort Knox-style security and was met by the
worried teachers. Little Anna was sleeping in the corner under some pink
covers and her twin sister Sofia was stroking her hair gently like a guardian
angel. I picked Anna up from the cot and she woke up startled but gave me

the most loving and warm smile to say she now felt safe. On our way out to the waiting car, we ran into Puk in the hallway just arriving after hearing the message on her voicemail. Anna was clearly distressed and in pain but very happy to see Mum also. We took her to the Marylebone Eye Hospital where we went straight to a small operating theatre.

As the doctor was getting ready to examine Anna, my mobile started ringing. I was about to turn it off when I noticed a Norwegian number on the display – it could only be about Aker Yards. Puk gave me a 'You are not seriously going to answer that' look as I excused myself and went to the corner of the room.

'Lars – this is Arne from DNB. Our analyst just found some news on Aker.'

'This is really not a good time,' I replied, while keen that it be good news.

'I think you'll want to hear this. It'll take a second?'

'OK, fire away.'

'Well, our analyst has found a covenant in the debt prospectus that requires Aker to have certain earnings. If they don't reach the stipulated level, the debt holders can demand full repayment. With the new profit warning this might well happen and we were not sure Aker could refinance with the uncertain prospects. That could bankrupt the firm,' Arne continued.

'I read that prospectus and thought this could only be an issue next year or the following,' I replied, aghast that the bad news just kept coming, but also pleased that I was fairly certain this must be wrong.

'He is just finding out for sure, but I thought you would want to know immediately,' said Arne.

The doctor had walked over and stood next to me with an annoyed look. Like an angry schoolteacher, he hissed: 'You can't use mobiles in here'. I thought, 'This guy is about to put instruments in my kid's eye. Better listen to him.' I gave the doctor a brief nod then half-turned away to tell Arne to send me an SMS if Aker hit 60 or if the company confirmed the debt prospectus issue, then hung up.

'Sorry about that . . . work stuff,' I said apologetically to nobody in particular.

'OK – perhaps we can carry on with the *business* of fixing your daughter's eye,' said the doctor, with evident disdain for the *b*-word. He thought it would be less traumatic for Anna if I rather than one of the staff held her down and forced her eye open, which I did. She gave me this look of, 'How could you do this to me, Dad?' as she struggled in vain to free herself. The doctor quickly identified the problem and removed a small metal object from Anna's right eye with one of the hospital's scary-looking instruments. The metal had been stuck on the inside of her eyelid and had been scratching the eyeball whenever Anna rubbed her eye. She immediately felt much better, even if at the age of almost three she could not find the words to say so. We were told that she had some nasty scratches on her eyeball which would heal with time, and the doctor gave her antibiotics.

We were in an emotionally hung-over state when we left the hospital. So many strong feelings of anxiety and relief in such a short time span but thrilled that our little daughter was going to be fine. 'With the neonatal ICU, colic, misdiagnosis of heart defect, meningitis threat, and now this, we must have had our share of bad luck,' said Puk, summarising the trials of our first two years as parents. 'Too right,' I thought.

Always one to put a positive spin on things, Puk seemed less concerned about the large drawdown at work. 'You constantly talked about wanting to either make the fund truly big time or fail while trying to do so. That was always going to mean things could go wrong quicker and if this leads to the closing of the fund it's probably better that you find out sooner, rather than spending the next several years with investors dying from boredom at too conservative returns.'

We returned from the hospital early enough in the day that I could have gone back to the office to survey the damage, but I did not have it in me.

22

A bad run

The Aker Yards debacle turned out to be the beginning of the end for Holte Capital. Since it was an isolated incident unrelated to any market trend, the stocks we were short as a hedge did not react negatively to the profit warning. Consequently, our hedges could not mitigate the loss at all. Despite this, we still felt that our protection against the industry and wider market made our general hedging policy sensible. Since we hedged against so many risks, we needed higher leverage in our trades to increase our overall returns. But when the hedges failed to work, we would be hit by the double pain of a non-working hedge and a large position, with a high number of shares in one company. By the time we unwound the Aker Yards trade, it had cost us almost 4 per cent in performance. Had this situation occurred in our first year of operations, when our leverage was much lower, the loss would have been less than 1 per cent and hardly worth mentioning.

After Aker Yards, we ran into the kind of dry spell where nothing really went our way. Two of our hedges in one trade decided to merge and the perceived synergies from the combination meant those stocks shot up far more than our long positions, so we incurred another loss. What we thought was Europe's cheapest and most conservative bank managed to disappoint, while its massively geared peers surged in value. We prided ourselves on our work in the insurance sector, but whereas we had previously felt our thorough financial analysis gave us an edge, we now found an ever larger disconnect between the value of those companies and the net assets they held against future insurance liabilities. In other circumstances, that kind of disconnect would present an opportunity to add to the positions, but at this stage of larger overall losses these additional ones were highly unwelcome.

One of the advantages of our trading policy had always been that the diversity of our trades ensured low correlation with each other. We hedged each trade so that we could make it neutral to markets, currencies and industries. The thinking was that if we could make 25–30 market-neutral trades, the portfolio of those trades should generate a unique return profile by combining these unrelated profit opportunities. If the timing of our large increase in risk was bad luck and not a reflection of bad investment management on our part, then the thinking appeared sound. Since Holte Capital's launch, about 70 per cent of our trades had been profitable. The losing 30 per cent did not lose more money than our winning 70 per cent made. Where we got hurt was in the high gearing of the fund at the time of our first significant drawdown. Part of being a good manager is obviously to know when to use leverage. But our change in risk profile had more to do with our strategic view to remedy an earlier far too conservative risk profile and get to a permanent higher level of gearing in the fund than a view of the market at the time.

By October our year-to-date return was down in the low double digits. I think this terminology is used by managers who don't want to say the actual numbers. Around 12 per cent. There – I said it. Over the past couple of months it had been a struggle to understand why more of our trades moved in the same direction at the same time than in the past even if they seemed to be correctly hedged. I would have endless discussions with our investors and ask if they were seeing anything in the market that could drive some of these dislocations, but we found nothing. One worry was if the large investors saw similar funds to ours in trouble. This could suggest that funds that were in our trades were forced to unwind positions as a result of investor redemptions, which might drive prices to worse levels and cause us a loss. But this did not seem to be the case.

In retrospect, there were probably a few things working against us at the same time:

- Our largest loss – Aker Yards – was a single event that could have happened regardless of what else happened in the market.

- With more than $1 billion invested in the market, we had more market hedges and we were exposed to the risk that the large cap names (or high market value companies) as a group would outperform the more illiquid mid-cap (small value) names. As a result, some of our apparently unrelated trades started to correlate. Bad.

- Value trap. We were long too many cheap names that nobody cared about. In the long run the value would be realised and share prices go up more than hedges. But as John Maynard Keynes observed, 'In the long run we are all dead.'

- In time, this bad run would have corrected itself. Using back-of-the-envelope calculations, the majority of trades would have returned to better levels after six months – but we weren't able to hold out that long.

- It was unfortunate that the regeared Holte Capital had a history of a very conservative return profile and an investor base that was unaccustomed to seeing larger red numbers from us. If we had been perceived as a higher-risk fund, those investors might not have panicked.

> If we had been perceived as a higher-risk fund, those investors might not have panicked.

Cascading investors

I felt tremendous responsibility for the people who worked for me and it was perhaps for their sake that I fought as hard as I did for our survival. We put together presentations to our investors about how, with the exception of Aker Yards, all our losses were unrealised and actually presented a fantastic investment opportunity. We all felt this was true, even if the 'it will come back' argument can only be deployed so many times. The investors seemed to want to believe that we would turn things around, but were rightly concerned not only with their own assessment of the situation, but also with what other investors were doing.

We had four investors with an average of $60 million invested in the fund, and a number of smaller investors. We knew that should one or two of the larger investors decide to pull out of the fund there could easily be a cascade effect in which the others would want to follow suit to avoid being the last man standing. There were a couple of reasons for this. The last investors in a fund often do worse in a shutdown than if they had pulled their assets earlier. Hedge funds that have to sell securities to meet redemption payments will tend to sell the liquid securities first – it is easier to do – and therefore often end up with a less liquid portfolio of assets for the remaining investors. Should the remaining investors then wish to unwind this less liquid portfolio, it can often lead to large losses, with a small number of investors each bearing a large share of the loss. By being among the first to redeem their investment from a fund, an investor can prevent this.

Another factor was that if two of the larger investors left the fund, the other two might fall foul of their internal rules for how large a fraction of a fund they could hold. This could lead to all four large investors leaving in short order, with all the smaller investors virtually certain to follow suit.

Most of our investors had been with us for years and I considered several of them good personal friends. We had no real secrets from them. They had all experienced several funds where dodgy dealings came to light once things turned bad or where undisclosed lack of liquidity positions made bad positions terrible. At Holte Capital they seemed relieved that there were no such skeletons in our closet. We were simply a fund going through a terrible run, and it was their job to understand the implications of this.

After the close of the market each day, I would retire to the conference room to speak to our investors. The design of our open-plan office with the glass conference room meant that everyone could see me talking and I would often look back at the anxious faces of my colleagues. I knew, and they knew, that their jobs depended on these crucial investor decisions.

One afternoon near the end of another difficult day in the markets, I had a conversation with Dan, a guy who represented one of the largest investors in the fund and had become quite a good friend. Dan was quick and to the point.

'There are people here,' said Dan, 'who want us to pull out and we are meeting the investment committee in an hour to decide.'

'All of it?' I queried.

'Yup – and I gotta tell you it is not looking good. Can you give me some ammo?'

I started to go through some of the trades and told him how I felt that these were temporary dislocations that would correct in the near term and how our drawdown was not in fact that massive for the higher volatility fund we had now become. I went back to the argument that, had we had the level of risk we have in the portfolio now since inception, our returns would have been exceptional and we had clearly become better and not worse investors over time: all things I believed to be 100 per cent true. Dan's response at the end of my little monologue surprised me.

'Lars, we are friends, right?'

'I guess so.'

Dan chuckled and began to explain why he thought I was different from most hedge-fund managers. 'You are not in love with it like some of the guys we see,' he said. 'And that can easily be a good thing. You don't fall in love with trades. People here also rate your intelligence right at the top among the managers.' Much as I like compliments, I suspected this was ominous.

'But I must say,' continued Dan, 'that in the time I have known you I have never more than now gotten the sense that your heart is not in it. It would take you one or two years to recover from this and start growing again, and I am not sure you are willing to do that. Nor am I sure that it is fair to ask your investors to continue if your heart is not fully in it. And that in turn is bound to affect the quality of your work.'

> 'You are not in love with it like some of the guys we see,' he said. 'And that can easily be a good thing. You don't fall in love with trades.'

This was painful. He was undoubtedly right, but I still tried to convince him otherwise – although I suspected my chances were slim. Dan said he would call me the next day about the outcome of the investment committee meeting. Next day? What felt like a life-or-death answer and we would casually be told tomorrow? But I knew that firms like Dan's typically had systems whereby we would receive a fax copy of the redemption request right after the decision was taken. So I quickly started stealing glances at the fax machine next to the printer. It was now the end of the trading day and the trade confirmations were starting to come in. I jumped every time the fax started to print out something new. Could this be our death notice? I would casually stroll past the fax machine and pick up the message. Phew. Another trade confirmation. 'Are you expecting something important?' Doriana asked me after I had made another couple of speedy walks across the floor. 'Not sure, to be honest,' I said. I did not want everyone to be on edge like me. If the dreaded redemption happened, I would rather assess the new situation first and then have a group meeting about it. I stayed at the office until 9pm and made another six trips to the fax machine. Another six trade confirmations. We were safe.

The following morning Doriana came by my desk. 'This fax came in for you overnight.' It was a redemption notice for the full investment. My heart sank and the noise around me became a blur. After that, everything seemed to happen very quickly. I felt it would be irresponsible not to tell the other larger investors that a significant investor had pulled out, also to reassure them that there were no business issues as a result. While they were keenly aware of our difficult position, it was no surprise when they told me this meant they too would have to consider whether they were going to stay in the fund. One or two even made remarks about me similar to Dan's.

We had a group meeting at which we discussed the implications of this large redemption. We could manage one, but if we received more there would be a stampede of exiting investors. In the days that followed, the whole office froze every time an investor called for me. Was this call the kiss of death or a simple request for an update? I could see the despair and concern on the faces of the team whenever Doriana told me there was an investor on the phone.

Within a couple of days it became clear that we had a stampede of investors wanting to leave. There were still a number of smaller investors I had not talked to as frequently who might well decide to stay in the fund; there was also my own capital, but I never really considered riding out the storm and continuing with the fund with whatever capital remained. Instead I called up all the investors who had not already put in a redemption notice and told them we would be returning all their capital. Although we gave a number of people their money back before they asked for it, I can't pretend anyone was begging me to continue to manage their money. They were not. Instead of leaving the last investors holding the bag with the most illiquid investments (of which there were very few – about 2 per cent of the portfolio), they were given their money back on the same terms as the larger redeeming investors left in the fund. It was all over.

23

Going home

Quiet anniversary

During the difficult final months of Holte Capital I kept in close touch with Brian, our former CFO. He knew how I felt, and would tell me what he thought, whether I wanted to hear it or not. The fund had its fifth anniversary on 1 November 2007. There were no celebrations. Brian sent me an email telling me not to forget what I had achieved, despite the recent difficulties. Had he asked me in 2002 if I expected the fund to see its fifth anniversary, I would have said no. We had clearly achieved a lot and experienced many things. I had also made a great deal of money. Not a bad outing overall, even as it became clear that we had not built anything of sustainable value. We would just be another footnote in the endless stories of hedge funds that come and go.

As a team there was no real drama. None of the analysts had done well that year and we all knew that this was the kind of industry where things are brilliant when all goes well, but that the flipside is a quick and merciless shutdown if things go badly. Considering the talents of the group, I felt fairly confident that they would all be able to get new jobs quickly and that their previous bonus payments made them financially secure for a good while. On the non-investing side, I knew that our new CFO Francois had the quality and connections to quickly move on and I planned to keep employing our office manager Doriana.

There were no recriminations. Everyone had seen this coming and we had often discussed how it would only take one investor pulling out to bring the house of cards tumbling down. Once I had told everyone about the redemptions we had received, there was no need to say more. One of the guys asked me if I might continue with a smaller fund and largely my own money, but otherwise everyone understood that this was the end of the road.

It was an odd feeling as the team started to leave. Over the years we had had very little staff turnover and had grown quite tight as a group. That it could be over in a matter of months seemed surreal – people hesitated and seemed unsure whether they should say 'goodbye' or 'see you soon' as they left with their boxes of personal belongings. Since I trusted that nobody would do anything untoward, everyone was allowed to keep their financial models and anything else that they wanted. There was no need for the brutal business of walking people to the elevator and asking for their passes, investment banking style.

It quickly became apparent how unsurprised our counterparties were by our sudden shutdown. I called around the 12–15 brokers we used the most to explain to them that we would not be doing much more business with them, but that we wished them luck and hoped to stay in touch. They had heard it a thousand times. Almost without fail they said: 'You'll be back before you know it – six months on the beach and the wife will kick you out.' I was equally certain this would not be the case and told them as much, to which they all said: 'That's what they all say.'

> 'I am too young to leave without a trace,' I said, while thinking that wherever I found myself next, I hoped it would be in something other than hedge funds.

One German broker said how strange he found it that people he would talk to daily could disappear from his life overnight. There were those who got fired or quit and never made it into another money management firm, but in some cases people just had enough and left without a trace. 'I am too young to leave without a trace,' I said, while thinking that wherever I found myself next, I hoped it would be in something other than hedge funds.

Other contacts such as lawyers, accountants, auditors, prime brokers and administrators tended to follow much the same routine:

1 Express surprise and sadness ('but you guys were such good clients').

2 Gauge how sorry the manager (Lars) is and give measured response (press '1' if manager seems happy, press '2' if manager is sad).

3 Offer help in any way with moving on to the next thing.

4 Say how you wish it was you going to the beach (many of these people sounded quite genuine, and indeed ended 2008 out of a job, with lots of time on their hands).

5 Plan to have lunch/coffee/dinner/pints that never actually happen.

6 Tell your boss that another sucker bites the dust, then have a cup of coffee and go back to your day. Next . . .

Many of these were genuinely caring and nice people, but this is business after all.

Our two prime brokers, Morgan Stanley and Credit Suisse, offered to help the team get new jobs through their 'talent introduction group'. They clearly have groups for everything. The talent introduction groups are used to connect clients with potential recruits and are a great way of finding people and jobs. Over the years we received endless résumés from those groups and two of our staff came that way. In time two from our team moved on this way.

The *Financial Times* and a couple of the industry rags asked for a comment. I chose not to. What was there to gain? The main surprise to me was that this was enough of a story that anyone would write about it. We were just another medium-sized London hedge fund with a bad run that was returning capital. We had lost investors some money in the past six months, but it was hardly a blow-up of newsworthy proportions. In the end I don't think anything was written apart from a little blurb in the trade magazine *Eurohedge*.

Counting the physical costs

From when I left New York in 1999 to the fall of 2007 I had not been to see a doctor. Like many other guys in their mid-30s I felt nothing was particularly wrong, even if it only took a glance in the mirror to see that things had gone downhill. On Puk's birthday in the fall she made me promise to go and have a full examination – one of those half-days of torture when they examine you all over and invariably find something wrong with you. And you pay a fortune for the pleasure of it all.

In my younger high-school and college days I fancied myself as an athlete and played several sports competitively. Even as late as in business school I ran the Boston marathon both years – the first time as a dare from the night before. Although it was hardly in a record-breaking time, I did manage to finish ahead of the guy wearing a diving bell and just behind someone carrying a waiter's tray.

I was a bit nervous before the day of the test. I searched the Internet for what was typically wrong with people like me, but found the reading too depressing and soon stopped. The first of the four examinations was with a young woman who had the look of, 'Thank God I get paid for this' as I took off my shirt. Sparing you the embarrassing details, very few corners were left unexamined and lots of tests were taken as four different doctors did their business. I am probably genetically blessed and there were no immediately serious concerns, but the doctors commented repeatedly that I had clearly seen high levels of stress for a significant period of time and my body bore the marks of an unhealthy diet and lack of exercise. One doctor suggested that if I kept up this lifestyle he reckoned I might reduce my life expectancy by 15 years. 'You're 35 years old but have the body of a 50-year-old, although you are not a smoker or heavy drinker and have healthy parents. If you continue like that something is going to give. We see so many people from the finance world whose later years are ruined by younger years of excess. Just don't say we didn't warn you.'

> The doctors commented repeatedly that I had clearly seen high levels of stress for a significant period of time and my body bore the marks of an unhealthy diet and lack of exercise.

Fair enough. I got the message. Back on that treadmill, fat boy.

In the years since I left business school in 1998 I had made the horrible mistake of keeping track of my weight. Every year in early January a reminder would spring up on my computer asking me how much I weighed, how I felt about it, and what my goals would be for the coming year. I would not recommend that to my worst enemy. My annual entries looked like I had hit the repeat button on the computer. Every year I had gained about 5lbs and every year the ambition the following year was to lose it again. Between the time I finished business school and the demise of Holte Capital, I gained 25lbs, which was hard to hide on a 5'11" body.

Turning off the lights

For the last three weeks before the final redemption date we had surrendered the office space and moved into the top floor of my Notting Hill house. There were only three of us left to do the final unwinding and sort out administrative things. The setting, with a view of Westbourne Grove, with über-trendy media folks walking the street, had a peculiar anti-start-up feeling to it. The set-up on the top floor with lots of computer screens and paper in messy piles everywhere seemed to belong to entrepreneurs starting out, not firms shutting down. Just as when we had started out, we had trouble getting the phone to work. We had come full circle, but this time there would be no photos of hopeful entrepreneurs hugging a company logo.

The last couple of months of unwinding the portfolio were tough, but each day I felt closer to the light at the end of the tunnel. We were determined to do things in the proper fashion and maintain good relations with the investors and counterparties. Every day was excruciating. There was nothing to gain, only damage to control. But with the end in sight it seemed bearable. Puk and I would spend the evenings planning the seven-week road trip we wanted to take from Miami to San Francisco with the kids after it was all done. After that we would spend the summer with the family on the beach in Denmark. Then, who knew?

The first of February 2008 was the first day of the rest of my life. There were no more outside investors and no positions that needed to be traded. We were done. Rather than going upstairs to turn on my computer and see what was happening in the market, I went for a walk in the rain and ended up at a café reading the sports pages for a couple of hours. My mind was not reflecting on the experiences of the past six years or what the future held. It was blank. Tired. I just wanted to read the sports pages to see how my favourite team, Queens Park Rangers, had acquitted themselves. I wanted to be left alone. After drinking my third cappuccino I went back outside and up the street to a Chinese herbal store. They offered neck and shoulder massages at £10 for 15 minutes. During the past stressful months I had had constant headaches from the tension in my shoulders and I hoped a massage could help me loosen up. It was time to start the healing process.

24

Rethinking Holte Capital

Our excuse

It seems that every collapsed hedge fund can explain how they actually did really well and either they were wildly unfortunate or their losses were someone else's fault. We are no different.

It is particularly laughable how many people put themselves in the category of: 'Can you believe it? XYZ happened – that is a one-in-a-million event.' Equally self-deluding are those who insist rather more pretentiously that they were the victims of a 'six-sigma event'. The only advantage of this expression is that it may scare away the follow-up question. Who wants to sound stupid by admitting that you don't know what 'six sigma' means even if the guy in front of you has just cost you a fortune? Sigma (standard deviation) is a measure of how frequent various outlying events (or numbers) are relative to an average occurrence. A six-sigma event is something that should happen so infrequently that you might have heard about a guy who had heard about a guy who knows someone that it happened to; and that should happen about every 100 years. Yet it seems to happen to every other hedge fund that loses a lot of money.

At Holte Capital our issue was somewhat different. We were hit by our first real drawdown at a time when we finally felt that we had taken our gearing up to a level where our returns would be appealing to a broad investor base. The risk levels were wrong for 90 per cent of the time Holte Capital was around. I have yet to hear anyone question the quality of our work, our ethics, our attempts to practise what we preached, our skill level, or that we were the right people to be making it happen; but again and again previous investors told me they wished we had taken more risk. Some have commented that we were in the top 5 per cent lowest-risk funds before we increased gearing – we were just not exciting enough.

In our first year of operations we were on average 70–80 per cent gross invested and we increased that steadily to be around 325 per cent on average in our fifth and last year. At the time of the Aker Yards profit warning we were approximately 350 per cent invested – our highest yet.

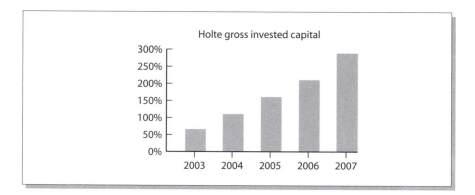

While a portfolio that is 350 per cent gross invested (your longs plus your shorts equal $350 for every $100 you have in the fund) seems highly geared, our conservative hedging profile actually necessitated this level of gearing to achieve the promised risk profile. Ever sceptical of throwing around standard deviation numbers – they can hide so many risks and often don't account for 'highly unlikely' events – we thought a risk profile with a standard deviation of 10–12 per cent would be acceptable to our investors. By contrast, we actually delivered a return profile with a standard deviation of 4 per cent, and we did not see anything internally to suggest there were hidden risks not expressed in the numbers.

To address our chronic underinvestment we tried to find the level of gearing at which our historical portfolio would have yielded a more satisfactory (higher) risk profile. We created a 'what if' sheet. The sheet showed what our net returns to the investors would have been at various levels of gross invested capital. We used the sheet to get a sense for what levels of risk our investors were happy with and came back every time with the answer: 'more risk'. Clearly they meant higher returns, but they were more than happy to see us increase the risk to achieve that. We had, after all, not had a down year in our five years.

So although we had returned around 7 per cent net to the investors per year we still felt we could explain why this was actually very good. The returns were achieved with little market correlation and very little risk, when interest rates were low. Of course our investors gave me the bored look of someone who is far too used to hearing excuses and even a bit of 'show me the money' attitude. And showing the money was exactly what we were trying to do when we got hit by our drawdown.

At a level of risk in line with 325–350 per cent gross invested, our yearly returns would have been around 18 per cent net to the investors, which was clearly excellent and with a standard deviation of only around 12 per cent. It was our firm internal belief that we should have raised our gearing all along, but better late than never. In 2006 we had a good year with nearly 15 per cent net returns and we saw no reason why we should not improve this as we increased risk further. I kept hammering home the point to our investors that most larger funds that have high return profiles do so with massive market exposures even if their illiquid portfolios allow them to avoid marking down securities in a down market and thus avoid showing their market exposure. At Holte Capital I felt our market exposure was much more limited, and the low correlation to the markets only made our risk-adjusted returns look even better. But again our investors said, 'That all sounds very good, Lars, but your talk will not fatten my bank account – returns will'.

By 2007 we felt this was our time. We had been frustrated that our low-risk profile hindered our growth to become a mega-fund, but it was not easy to increase risk so dramatically in a short period of time, as our existing investors all had to be fully informed and on board, otherwise they might have felt they bought a very low-volatility product and feel misled at it changing into a high-volatility one. But in the late spring of 2007 we were finally at the gearing levels commensurate with the high-performance fund we wanted to become.

Anyway, as I said, everyone's got an excuse. Now you know ours.

Conclusions

The fall of 2008 and spring of 2009 was certainly a curious time to write about my time in the hedge-fund industry. I was constantly aware of friends whose worlds were collapsing one down-tick at a time. Although I was certainly not jealous of them, I remember regretting that Holte Capital did not have a chance to test its collective skills in perhaps the most challenging market for a generation. Instead, I was planning to tell the story of one firm in an industry that many people expected to self-destruct. The promised protection against falling markets had failed to materialise in an apparently collective bottomless fall. It seemed as if there would be far more interesting stories to tell than the first-hand account of the rise and fall of a medium-sized London-based hedge fund, run by yet another young guy who thought he was the next master of the universe.

My reflections on my years at Holte Capital come under four headings.

1 **It was a job worth doing.** The work we did at Holte was really interesting and we believed we had a genuine edge in our analysis. Without institutional bonds to put restrictions on what we could analyse, we were free to explore what we considered most worthy of study and had the greatest prospect of profit. This kind of freedom from investment restrictions is one of the things hedge-fund managers like most about their jobs.

> This kind of freedom from investment restrictions is one of the things hedge-fund managers like most about their jobs.

When I look back at the period when I ran Holte Capital I feel tremendously lucky to have managed a portfolio at a time when the hedge-fund industry was undergoing tumultuous and rapid change. The boundaries of the possible seemed to be rewritten every year. Having seen many hedge funds go through the same rough and tumble we did, I now know that I was extremely fortunate with the most honest and smart co-workers and investors I could have hoped for – the lack of which sinks far greater talents than mine.

My greatest source of pride and pleasure from my time with Holte Capital was the thrill of being a true entrepreneur. We took the business from nothing to the point where we were throwing around $1 billion within five years without any kind of institutional backing. We were successful entrepreneurs in a fiercely competitive sector and that was an incredible feeling. Through skill, hard work, and a healthy dose of luck we had built a thriving profitable business. Many people in finance made or managed much more money than we did, but I am very proud of the success we achieved.

2 **We made plenty of mistakes.** In hindsight, of course, there are many things I would have done differently at Holte Capital. I wish we had taken more risk in the portfolio – our conservative gearing did not allow our investors to gain the higher returns that the quality of our analysis warranted. I also wish I had been able to see the longer-term picture without constantly worrying about the fund's returns over the next days or weeks. I wish I had been able to recognise that without a more healthy work/family balance there was no way I could have sustained either in the long run; this probably made me view the firm as more of a sprint than the marathon that most successful investment firms turn into. I should have been better at occasionally looking up from my desk and appreciating where we had reached, instead of always worrying about the next potential problem. There are employees, counterparties and investors to whom I wish I had shown more gratitude, either financially or verbally. The list goes on . . .

3 **There is nothing intrinsically wrong with hedge funds**. This is an industry that attracts some of the best minds in finance and gives them a wide mandate to generate returns that greatly enhance the risk/return profile of any portfolio. If they do well, they are amply rewarded, and if they fail, they are fired.

While the hedge-fund industry was still a fairly small sector that profitably exploited selected pockets of market inefficiencies, the premise worked. As the number of hedge funds exploded to the near 10,000 in existence today, I think too many mediocre managers were paid too much for the industry to make sense to the end investor (like Mrs Straw, mentioned earlier). There is still undoubtedly world-class talent adding a great amount of value, but the explosion in numbers of managers and assets managed means that the value added for investors by the industry today is questionable. Does it make enough money to justify its fees?

Even if you take the best qualified analysts with the best access to information and resources, it is very hard to beat markets after fees consistently over time. Particularly towards the end of my time at Holte Capita, I had increasingly reached this view and felt slightly dejected as a result. It seems to me that in order to be a successful manager over a long period of time, you have to love investing money, regardless of the income you get from it; you also have to firmly believe you can beat markets. Otherwise the work will become soul-destroying as you begin to question the wider benefits of what you are doing. Perhaps I had subconsciously reached that point towards the end.

In the aftermath of the large bank bailouts of 2008 and 2009 a general consensus seemed to emerge that people in finance are overpaid. In many cases I agree, but not across the board. Some financiers manage and control vast amounts of money. If you accept that there is skill involved in this work (which you should do if you invest with them), then the sheer magnitude of money being managed means that the best managers deserve to gain substantially from having assumed such responsibility. By contrast, mediocre financiers clearly do not deserve to be paid large amounts for adding very little value.

4 **Money matters, but only up to a point.** When I was at business school, people always seemed to lecture us students to follow our dreams and pursue the careers we were most interested in, regardless of the latest fashion or that career's income potential. I remember this annoying me. I thought this often ignored the realities of most people's lives. Many people had debts to pay off, young families to support, or mortgage payments to meet. These obligations meant that a pay cheque came first, lofty dreams second, in my opinion.

Recently I caught myself giving that same advice to a business-school student. When I told him that the most important thing was that he did something he truly loved and felt passionate about, I saw his frustrated look that seemed to say: 'That's easy for you to say.' He was right. It is easy for me to say – now.

I have been incredibly lucky. I have a loving family and great friends. I have made enough money not to have to worry about that, and at 38 years of age I am in decent health. I am happy, and I now have plenty of time to spend with my wife and two daughters. After finishing up at Holte Capital, I joined a couple of boards, including that of a hedge fund. I really enjoy this work. But it is not a full-time future occupation, and I am hungry for more.

Are hedge funds really safe places for your money?

An alternative to the alternatives

As my encounter with Mrs Straw and the subsequent calculations convinced me, fees in hedge funds and associated affiliates like funds of funds are too high to be sustainable in the long run. Too many well-fed mouths have been fed by the accumulated fees to the point where Mrs Straw will eventually be left wondering where all the money from her supposedly good investments has gone. Adding to the high fees the fact that many funds are exposed to market fluctuations that investors could get far more cheaply elsewhere, investors are effectively charged even more for the additional value (alpha) generated by the hedge-fund manager.

> Fees in hedge funds and associated affiliates like funds of funds are too high to be sustainable in the long run.

The fact that there are too many hedge funds in the world today and trillions of dollars managed by them does not mean that individual funds can't have genuine edge and offer real value, but it does mean that in aggregate the industry doesn't add enough value to justify the high fees. So unless an investor has an unusual ability to sort though the fancy presentations and track records of a long list of tempting hedge-fund managers who are undoubtedly experts at explaining why their product has unheard-of edge, he should probably stay away altogether.

But nor does this mean we should keep our money in the bank or sewn into our mattresses. If you have found a money manager who has the ability to either pick the direction of the markets or consistently beat them after fees, by all means exploit that advantage for all it is worth. Take your investment and use debt (if you can find any) to increase your exposure to this competitive edge and you will be assured large riches if you are indeed correct. For those without this insight or access to a manager with this insight, we will have to consider far more mundane alternatives.

If you are ready to acknowledge that not only do you not have edge in the market, but you also don't know anyone who you are convinced has edge, you are already doing well. Conceding edge means that you should not pay anyone a lot of money to manage your assets and this alone will serve you very well in the long run.

The acknowledged lack of edge in the markets does not mean that you should not invest in the markets. Notwithstanding 2008, markets do tend to go up over time and since missing out on investing in the markets means having your money in unexciting deposit accounts, wider stock markets certainly offer interesting investment opportunities. The key to investing in the stock markets is to know your attitude towards risk and have a good idea about the time horizon for your investment. If you have $105 and need $100 for heart surgery next year you should not invest in risky assets like the stock markets, but if you have a ten-year or longer horizon you can accept more risk in your investment strategy and should not have your money earning interest that only keeps pace with inflation.

Where to invest

Along with stock-market futures, index products such as Vanguard tracker funds or the many ETFs (exchange traded funds) offer the cheapest access to the various indices they represent. If we buy 20 mutual funds that try to beat the S&P500 index, the chances are that, on average, they will underperform the index by approximately their fees. The fees in these mutual funds vary but, including trading and related expenses, come to around 1.5–2 per cent per year, compared with tracker fund fees of roughly 0.2

per cent per year. Over time the difference between the two will matter greatly. If we invest $100,000 and earn approximately a 10 per cent gross return over a ten-year period, the net difference between the two will be about $34,000. For an individual, that might buy a new car. For a university endowment, it could mean launching a couple of new departments. For a large pension fund, the difference could amount to billions. And because you did not pay a lot of money to people you did not think had edge anyway.

It gets trickier and far more interesting when we ask: why restrict ourselves to the S&P500 or whatever happens to be the local market? For many investors, investing in their local market gives them a sense of being able to track the markets and they appreciate the comfort that comes from that. But why just that market? Suppose we take an investment in the S&P500 and reinvest it to split it between the S&P500, Eurostoxx50, and the Japanese index (Nikkei), all in local currencies? We would be better off as diversification increases. The key to understanding this advantage is the *correlation* between the various markets. Remember that word – correlation. It is one of the most important, yet overused, terms in finance.

> Remember that word – correlation. It is one of the most important, yet over-used, terms in finance.

The thing with correlation is that it gives an idea of how markets move relative to each other. Two markets with a correlation of zero will move independently of each other while two markets with a correlation of 1 will move in perfect lockstep. In an ideal world, we would invest in a number of markets with zero correlation. Then the expected yearly return of each market would enable us to virtually guarantee positive overall returns every year, even though individual markets might have down years. In the real world, things are unfortunately not that easy.

Some markets correlate more than others. Typically, neighbouring countries correlate – Holland and Belgium will correlate more highly than either of those countries will with New Zealand, even if the industries and economies are similar. But while Norway is a long way from Kuwait, the markets of both countries are highly oil-dependent, and correlate as a result. The market for corporate and particularly emerging-market debt across the globe will tend to correlate as the investors in those markets are dominated by large interdependent financial institutions, as painfully

2008. Finally, the whole world depends on the US markets – as fully proved during the 2008 meltdown. It is difficult enough y assess past correlations, so it's hardly surprising that we run into trouble when what we are looking for is not a measure of the past but an estimate of future correlation. Then we must try to gauge how we can get the most diversification from investing in a combination of markets. Past correlation data may provide a good guide for estimating future correlation, but counting on those numbers alone to make precise forecasts would be unwise; the world and correlations change constantly.

Creating a diversified portfolio

What we are trying to do is to create a portfolio of well-diversified liquid markets across the world in a way that is cheap to put together and where we have a reasonable estimate of the risk we are undertaking. While investing assets such as real estate or private equity may be appealing, they are less liquid and often come with high fees. Instead we should focus on liquid debt (corporate and government) and equity markets across the world where we have an expectation of positive returns (as we do in most markets), an idea of how the tradeable values move relative to other markets (correlation), and a reasonable estimate of the risk of each individual investment (volatility). In finance theory, what we are trying to do is to create a real-life practical investment on the 'efficient market frontier'. For the very technical, there are two areas where we differ from traditional finance theory: we will not be investing according to market sizes (that would lead to disproportionate investments where capital markets make up a large percentage of GDP (gross domestic product) and leave us with mainly the USA and Western Europe), and we do not think the expected returns across the world strictly follow the methodology of the Capital Asset Pricing Model (CAPM). This would suggest that the risk premium in smaller markets is barely above zero.

The main concern with a broadly diversified portfolio is that diversification gives a false sense of security. When the shit hits the fan, all markets act as one and our fancy charts go out the window, along with correlation assumptions, especially in emerging markets. During the 2008 meltdown, no markets were spared, just as in September 2001 when they all took a hit at the same time. Imagine disasters like a particularly virulent form of SARS, widespread armed conflict, or other yet unimaginable disasters, and it is hard to imagine a broad index anywhere in the world that would not be hurt. In that scenario, our chart would have done us much more harm than good. We would have taken on greater risk, thinking that the diversification had lowered our risk, but when we most needed protection there would be none as all the individual markets would fall simultaneously. In technical terms, the correlations would have increased dramatically, as would the expected risk (standard deviation) in each of the individual markets and consequently for our portfolio as a whole.

To make this diversified portfolio thinking truly robust, we need to protect ourselves against disaster scenarios. We could do so by buying insurance against significant price drops in the stock market – known in the business as out-of-the-money put options. It is in very bad markets that the correlation between markets increases most substantially; those are the very markets we protect ourselves against with out-of-the-money puts. By eliminating the return periods with highest correlation through the protection, we reduce the net correlation in the remaining periods and increase our expected returns. Of course the purchase of puts will dampen our upside since protection can be costly, but investing along the efficient frontier (i.e., investing to maximise expected returns for a given level of risk) will probably more than make up for this option cost. It will also protect us against the kind of meltdown we have seen in 2008 or can envisage in the future. We can partly finance the costs of put protection by selling out-of-the-money call options. There is, somewhat less convincing, evidence that markets also correlate more highly in rising markets, leaving the more normal markets in between with lower expected correlations.

There is a point at which insurance against market falls becomes prohibitively expensive (in the fall of 2008, standard deviation traded near 80 per cent), but in those cases the indicated volatility level is effectively saying that the world markets will behave as one – correlations among different markets will be near their peak. Since correlations can hardly go up from there (markets can't be better than perfectly correlated) this is really like saying you are buying protection against one giant market and the protection will only be as effective as if you had bought it for one market only. Admittedly this is when this investment strategy adds the least value and is only about as effective (but no worse) than investing in a single market. At other times our out-of-the-money protection would serve the double purpose of protecting not only against large drops in the value of our assets, but also against all market correlations going up (what you really want is options against correlations going up, but those don't exist in the market).

If we have only bought general indices on stocks and bonds, we have not paid anyone a ton of money to be smart about beating the markets (since we don't think it can consistently be done after fees). Consequently, our portfolio is cheaply constructed. Our portfolio consists of a series of index futures, exchange-traded funds (ETFs), and broad indices of corporate and government bonds, plus some market protection. Over a five-to-ten-year time horizon, the low cost of the portfolio alone should cause us to outperform the active managers who are weighed down both by fees and by investing in a narrower subset of the market than our broadly diversified and downside-protected portfolio.

A few summarising thoughts:

- If you accept that market direction can't be consistently predicted, you should not try to do so or pay anyone a lot of money to try to do this on your behalf. If you accept active management, you implicitly accept the corresponding high fees and expenses.

- It makes sense to diversify your portfolio to avoid dependence on one market, region or asset class, while protecting yourself in a case of extreme distress (think fall of 2008 or worse) by buying out-of-the-money put options. These options also reduce the average correlation of your investment assets and thus increase your expected returns.

- You need a longer time horizon. In any one year this portfolio would probably beat the average performance of the markets it invested in, although if your local alternative was the world's best-performing market, our alternative portfolio would underperform that year. But over the longer term our portfolio should beat individual local markets as short-term local outperformance will be bettered by the risk-adjusted diversification we provide by investing in multiple markets with low correlation.

- You need to think about the risk you want to take and adjust the gearing of the portfolio accordingly.

- Although the portfolio would not be static, there would be fairly little trading and the costs and fees could be kept very low as a result – besides, it is fairly cheap to buy whole markets through ETFs or futures.

As far as I have been able to find out, there are few money-management firms that do the kind of investing described above. When I asked a former professor of mine at Harvard, he said that for whatever reason the world does not seem to value this kind of investing very highly. Increasing amounts of money are invested in index funds like Vanguard, but taking that a step further and picking broad arrays of indices has for whatever reason not been something a lot of people do or are willing to pay a lot for. This is probably because anyone who can convince people to let them manage their money would prefer to claim higher fees for doing so, and would not want clients to allocate money to an index-fund product that might charge a mere 0.2 per cent per year or less. There is more money to be made from active management or convincing people to invest in fancier products like hedge funds or private equity. The above is highly unsexy as it does not claim to be able to beat the market or be particularly brilliant at financial analysis. Perhaps calling this type of investment the Ryanair or WalMart of finance is an appropriate analogy.

After making my own scepticism about the high levels of fees floating around the financial system clear to anyone who cares to listen (and many that don't), I often get asked how I think people should invest their money. The above may sound like financial mumbo-jumbo, but it is eminently practicable in the real world – sort of a real and practical adapted version of a capital asset pricing model (CAPM), with protection. You buy a portfolio of cheap stock-index funds, corporate and government debts and put it together in a portfolio that you protect through out-of-the-money put options. The calculations behind this project might be somewhat complex, with many indices involved, but relying too much on high-level calculations also misses the point that model calculations are only as good as the assumptions you put in, and that the expectation of great precision is misleading. My mother has often asked me what she should do with her savings or pension fund, and in my mind this kind of product is the answer. It is cheap, well diversified but protected against massive downside, and will probably outperform alternatives in the long run. It seems to me that this project deserves further exploration.

Index